D0344214

SALADS

HAMLYN
new
COOKERY

SALADS

LYN RUTHERFORD

PHOTOGRAPHY BY GRAHAM KIRK

First published in Great Britain in 1995
by Hamlyn
an imprint of Reed Consumer Books Limited
Michelin House, 81 Fulham Road, London SW3 6RB
and Auckland, Melbourne, Singapore and Toronto

Copyright © 1995 Reed International Books Limited

All rights reserved. No part of this publication may be
reproduced, stored in a retrieval system or transmitted in
any form or by any means, electronic, mechanical, photo-
copying, recording or otherwise, without the permission of
the publisher.

ISBN 0 600 58335 X

A CIP catalogue record for this book is available from the
British Library

Produced by Mandarin Offset
Printed in Hong Kong

ACKNOWLEDGEMENTS

Art Director Jacqui Small
Executive Art Editor Penny Stock
Designers Barbara Zuniga and Ben Barrett
Commissioning Editor Nicky Hill
Editors Jenni Fleetwood and Sasha Judelson
Production Controller Melanie Frantz
Photographer Graham Kirk
Step-by-step Photography by Jonathan Lovekin
Home Economist Lyn Rutherford
Stylist Helen Payne

NOTES

Both metric and imperial measurements have been given
in all recipes. Use one set of measurements only and not a
mixture of both.

Standard level spoon measurements are used in all recipes.
1 tablespoon = one 15 ml spoon
1 teaspoon = one 5 ml spoon

Eggs should be size 3 unless otherwise stated.

Milk should be full fat unless otherwise stated.

Pepper should be freshly ground black pepper unless
otherwise stated.

Fresh herbs should be used unless otherwise stated. If
unavailable use dried herbs as an alternative but halve
the quantities stated.

Ovens should be preheated to the specified temperature
– if using a fan-assisted oven, follow the manufacturer's
instructions for adjusting the time and the temperature.

CONTENTS

INTRODUCTION

Salads offer unlimited scope to the cook's imagination, with a huge variety of ingredients: salad leaves, vegetables, herbs, fruit, fish and meat, pasta and rice, nuts and seeds, even flowers. Anything goes, to create a stylish side dish or starter, or a lunch or supper dish in its own right.

Gone are the days when salad was the dull slimmer's option – although if you are counting calories you should go easy on the dressing – today's salads are a riot of colours, textures and flavours, packed with positively healthy ingredients.

Salads certainly need not be reserved for summer, when they are seen as cold food for when it's too hot to cook, although many of my ideas require no cooking. Salads can be served hot, with a sizzling dressing poured over the leaves at the last minute, or warm, perhaps with freshly cooked root vegetables left to absorb the flavours of aromatic oils for 15-20 minutes.

It would be a pity not to make good use of the produce available from your greengrocer or your garden to reflect the changing seasons in your salads. I have devoted a whole chapter to discovering the delights of winter – golden swede, earthy beetroot, parsnips, baby turnips, celeriac, Jerusalem artichokes. With all cooking the finished dish is only as good as the ingredients in it – this is especially true of salads. Choose bright, perky leaves and herbs, crisp seasonal vegetables and fruits that are in their ripest, most flavoursome condition. Use produce when it is at its best: if something is not available in its prime, substitute another ingredient.

I hope that this will be more than just a recipe book, and will prove a source of inspiration throughout the year. Be adventurous in choosing your ingredients and be bold and creative when putting them together.

SALADS AND HEALTH
There are many healthy benefits from eating plenty of salad. Nutritionists recommend that we eat at least 5 helpings a day of vegetables or fruit. Making a salad into a meal can provide 2 or 3 helpings of raw and lightly cooked leaves, fruit and vegetables, with their abundant vitamins and minerals.

Most salads should be prepared as near to serving time as possible – not only are they at their crispest and brightest, they will also be more nutritious, as vitamins can be destroyed as soon as leaves and vegetables are cut. Do not allow leaves to soak in water – vitamin C is water-soluble and easily lost. Rinse the leaves if necessary, then dry in a salad spinner or gently shake off excess moisture in a clean tea towel.

BASIC INGREDIENTS
Today's supermarkets and greengrocers boast an ever-increasing range of fresh produce. Salads provide a great opportunity to experiment with some of the unusual fruits and vegetables that occasionally appear in supermarkets, such as yellow tomatoes, courgette flowers and dwarf pattypan squash (sometimes known as custard marrows). The recipes in this book are meant as suggestions upon which you can build your own salads.

SALAD LEAVES
Even the basic lettuce is now available in an enormous array of colours, shapes and sizes, with different textures and tastes. A far cry from the limp lettuce that was ubiquitous 20 years ago, it is now easy to buy robust leaves such as cos (or romaine) and iceberg lettuce that welcome hot dressings, wilting gently without dissolving into an unappealing mess.

Tender young spinach leaves are particularly versatile: when used completely raw they are almost squeaky to bite, with a delicious, almost peppery taste; when served with hot grilled cheese or bacon they retain their shape well.

The palette of colour has broadened to take in the bright pinkish red of radicchio and the subtle maroons and bronze tones of red oakleaf lettuce (feuille de chêne), four seasons (quattro stagioni) and the frilly-leaved lollo rosso.

While some leaves bring little more than eye-appeal, others have distinctive flavours of their own. Escarole, frisé, chicory and radicchio are appetizingly bitter, just waiting to meet a tasty dressing, while the small, peppery leaves of watercress and rocket (also known as roquette and arugula) form a lovely contrast to the sweetness of squid or prawns.

Don't forget that some common plants have intriguing flavours – such as the tangy dandelion and peppery nasturtium – and can bring a new dimension to your salads.

A mixture of leaves makes for a wonderful contrast of flavours as well as a very attractive salad.

VEGETABLES AND FRUIT

To make more of a simple salad, try adding raw or blanched vegetables such as broccoli, cauliflower or mangetout. Their distinctive flavours and crisp textures will give added interest and nutritional value.

Think about whether you are aiming for a salad of bright contrasting colours, with tomatoes, beetroot, red cabbage or red onion standing out against a green background, or whether the rest of the meal calls out for a more harmonious collection of greens, for example with courgettes, cucumber, avocado and celery.

Selections of cultivated mushrooms (brown chestnut mushrooms, yellow and pale grey oyster mushrooms, meaty shiitake), now sold in many supermarkets, add earthy tastes and melting or chewy textures. In autumn you can include wild mushrooms, but be careful to identify them correctly, as some can be toxic when raw.

Fresh fruit, such as strawberries, apples or oranges, cut into slices or bite-sized pieces, coated in dressing and tossed with the other ingredients, can make a salad more substantial and help to emphasize other seasonal touches.

HERBS

I consider herbs, ideally picked fresh from the garden or window box, an almost indispensable addition to my salads. As attractive and fresh-looking garnishes, they can be chopped finely to give an even peppering of green, dotted about the plate as torn leaves, or presented in generous bunches. Some herbs, such as basil, mint and sage, have robust flavours that should be taken into consideration when composing a salad or

making a dressing; others, such as chervil, have subtler tastes.

EDIBLE FLOWERS

It's easy to make a salad look appetizing, either by choosing ingredients with contrasting colours, or by adding highlights in the form of edible flowers. These are now available from many supermarkets, but there is nothing to stop you picking them fresh from your garden or window box. They contribute little in the way of flavour, tending to be rather bland, but amply make up for this in the visual appeal of their jewel-like colours. Among the many flowers that you can eat are nasturtiums, rose petals, violas, pansies, heartsease and marigold petals (use pot marigolds, or Calendula, rather than the bedding or African marigolds, Tagetes) not forgetting the bright tiny flowers of many herbs, such as basil, chives, marjoram, oregano, thyme and borage.

DRESSINGS

The dressing is what really brings a salad together, marrying its separate ingredients into a harmonious whole. The simplest of dressings consist of little more than a flavoursome oil, perhaps with a sprinkling of salt, a twist of the pepper grinder and a squeeze of lemon juice.

Throughout the book I have given recipes for some distinctive dressings, which need not be confined to salads, but can also be served with grilled fish, poultry and meat. I have suggested particular combinations of oils and vinegars with certain salads, but these are not rigid rulings – half the fun of salad-making is in creating a dressing to suit your individual palate and mood.

Although there are plenty of ready-prepared dressings in the shops, by making your own you are not only creating something unique, you also have the satisfaction of knowing that it is free from artificial stabilizers, emulsifiers and other chemicals. I always feel it is best to make dressings fresh when you need them, taking inspiration from the salad ingredients.

OILS

The best of the powerfully flavoured oils are extra-virgin olive oil, walnut oil and hazelnut oil. Nut oils tend to become rancid with storage, so buy small bottles and use them within a month or two. Sesame oil has a very distinctive, sweet, nutty taste – use it sparingly, perhaps with a dash of soy sauce, to add an evocative Chinese flavour to salads made from bean sprouts, Chinese leaves, shellfish or duck.

Hot, spicy oils, sometimes sold as pizza dressings, are sold in some delicatessens and supermarkets, but you can make your own by gently heating a little olive oil with a few dried red chillies, leaving it to infuse overnight, then straining it into a clean jar or bottle, perhaps adding a few sprigs of herbs such as rosemary, which will gradually permeate the oil with their flavours.

Use blander oils – sunflower, groundnut, grapeseed, light olive oil – for dressings with other strong flavourings such as vinegars, herbs and fruit, and also for making mayonnaise. Good-quality mayonnaise can be bought ready made, but some brands are excessively sweet, bitter or rich, and can spoil a meal with unwelcome 'chemical' tastes. Mayonnaise is not difficult to prepare (although it requires a little patience, see pages 9 and 15), and you can make it exactly as you prefer, either full-flavoured, using a rich olive oil, or a lighter version with sunflower oil. Add lemon, pepper, garlic and herbs to suit the salad.

VINEGARS

To counteract the smoothness of the oil, a dressing usually includes a note of acidity: basic vinaigrette usually includes 3 or 4 parts oil to 1 part vinegar. Lemon or lime juice give a pleasant tang, or choose from a range of vinegars to contribute their own subtle flavours. Cider, white wine, red wine, sherry, tarragon and raspberry vinegars are widely available; balsamic vinegar, matured in wooden casks, can be expensive,

PREPARING A CRAB
1 *Pull off the claws and legs. Crack (do not crush) with a mallet; extract the meat.*

2 *Prise away the central body section. Discard the feathery whitish gills. Pick the white meat out of the hard sections.*

3 *Discard the head sac from the main shell, then scoop out and reserve the firm white meat and the soft brown meat.*

MAKING MAYONNAISE
(See page 15 for the basic recipe.)
1 *Put the yolks and mustard in a bowl.*

2 *Add the vinegar and seasoning, beat until smooth, then add the oil, a drop at a time, beating constantly.*

3 *When the mixture begins to thicken, pour in the oil in a thin stream, still beating constantly to blend in the oil.*

but a little of its rich, sweet and sour flavour goes a long way.

You can make your own special vinegars by slipping a few sprigs of fresh herbs (e.g. rosemary, thyme) or a few cloves of garlic into the bottle, or by macerating lightly crushed fruit such as blackberries in wine vinegar for 3-4 days, then straining it through a fine sieve, boiling it up and rebottling it. Flavoured vinegars also make great presents for foodie friends.

SALADS ON THE MENU
The traditional place of salads on the menu varies from country to country. In France, for example, a simple green salad may be served as a "refresher" course, with or after the cheese, and before pudding. There is a growing fashion to serve salad after the main course of a meal, whether or not vegetables have been served as well. This can lighten the meal and act as a source of refreshment to the palate before pudding,

or alternatively it can lead subtly on to the next course, be it cheese or fresh fruit.

Some years ago the style of cooking known as *nouvelle cuisine* introduced the *salade tiède*, or warm salad, often served as a sophisticated first course or light main meal. The focal point of the warm salad may be grilled goats' cheese, sautéed scallops, duck breast, bacon and walnuts or chicken livers.

The classic English crab salad (see left for tips on preparing a freshly boiled crab) is a good example of how a little protein can transform a salad into the perfect light lunch or supper. This book gives plenty of other suggestions in the chapters on Fish and Seafood, Meat and Poultry, with my own variations on popular dishes, from a platter of cold meats and coronation chicken to a salad version of duck with oranges and a tasty Indonesian salad with spicy peanut dressing.

The Greek 'village' salad not only epitomizes the summer food of the Mediterranean at its best, it too is a complete meal in itself, with its juicy tomatoes, cool cucumber, bitter black olives and fresh herbs, topped with crumbly feta cheese.

Vegetarian sources of protein, such as eggs and cheese, can make a salad into a satisfying one-course meal, and a separate chapter, Pasta and Grains, is devoted to more substantial additions: pasta, rice and other grains, and pulses such as lentils and dried or canned beans.

Croûtons, too, can add bulk to a salad, as well as a crunchy texture. They can be fried in oil and butter (see page 23) or flavoured with garlic salt (see page 18).

Salads that can be prepared in advance are a marvellous solution when entertaining more than just a few people. Serve a good selection, each with a different emphasis and dressing, to cater for all tastes.

Cottage Garden Salad with Strawberries

This salad was concocted with ingredients from an English country cottage garden – cultivated and wild edible leaves, herbs and glorious summer strawberries.

about 250 g/8 oz mixed salad leaves
(e.g. nasturtium, dandelion, rocket, escarole, oak leaf, salad burnet)
handful of fresh herb sprigs, with flowers
(e.g. fennel, chives, dill, mint)
250 g/8 oz small strawberries, hulled
1 quantity Yogurt Dressing (see page 38) or
Tarragon and Orange Dressing (see page 18)
salt and pepper

1 Tear all the leaves into fairly large pieces and put in a salad bowl or on individual plates. Scatter over the herbs.
2 Halve the strawberries, or leave them whole if very small. Add to the salad with a little salt and pepper.
3 Spoon the chosen dressing over the salad and toss lightly. Serve at once.

Serves 4-6
Preparation time: 10 minutes

Wilted Salad with Cheese and Sun-dried Tomatoes

Wafer-thin shavings of cheese melt into this salad when the hot dressing is added.

1 small cos lettuce, separated into
    leaves
about 50 g/2 oz rocket
½ head of radicchio, separated into
    leaves
125 g/4 oz cheese (e.g. Gruyère,
    Emmental or hard goats' cheese)
5 tablespoons olive oil
1 garlic clove, chopped
4 spring onions, chopped
6 sun-dried tomatoes preserved in oil,
    drained and sliced
2 tablespoons balsamic vinegar
salt and pepper
2 tablespoons pine nuts, toasted
    (optional)

1 Tear the salad leaves into bite-sized pieces and place in a shallow serving bowl. Using a cheese slicer or vegetable peeler, shave the cheese into wafer-thin slices and scatter over the salad.
2 Heat the oil in a frying pan. Add the garlic and cook over medium-high heat for 1 minute. Do not allow the garlic to brown. Stir in the spring onions and sun-dried tomatoes; cook for 1-2 minutes to heat through, then remove the pan from the heat.
3 Stir the balsamic vinegar into the pan, with salt and pepper to taste. Spoon the mixture over the salad. Serve at once, sprinkled with toasted pine nuts, if liked.

Serves 4
Preparation time: 15 minutes
Cooking time: 2-3 minutes

Mozzarella Salad with Pesto Dressing

Bocconcini are miniature balls of mozzarella cheese. They are sometimes available from supermarkets and Italian delicatessens, but if you cannot obtain them you can use regular mozzarella cut into cubes for this salad.

1 cos or other crisp green lettuce,
   separated into leaves
1 small head of frisé
250 g/8 oz bocconcini or diced
   mozzarella
1 red onion, chopped
salt and pepper
½ quantity Pesto Dressing (see page 40)
fresh basil leaves and sprigs of
   oregano, to garnish

1 Tear the salad leaves into bite-sized pieces and arrange on a platter or shallow serving dish. Scatter the bocconcini or diced mozzarella over the leaves and sprinkle with the chopped red onion. Add salt and pepper to taste.
2 Spoon the dressing over the mozzarella and sprinkle the salad with the fresh basil leaves and oregano to garnish.

Serves 4
Preparation time: 10 minutes

Caesar Salad

My good friend Jess prepares this, the ultimate Caesar salad, with huge, hot, buttery croûtons and a creamy dressing that stings with garlic. Vegetarians can replace the anchovies with smoky slivers of grilled yellow pepper. I'm not even sure which version I prefer.

1 cos lettuce, separated into leaves
1 x 50 g/2 oz can anchovies in olive oil, drained
1 small rustic white loaf (uncut)
75 g/3 oz butter, melted
3 tablespoons freshly grated Parmesan cheese

DRESSING:
5 tablespoons Mayonnaise (see right)
4-5 tablespoons water
1-2 garlic cloves
3 tablespoons finely grated Parmesan cheese
coarse sea salt and pepper

1 Start by making the dressing. Put the mayonnaise in a small bowl and stir in enough of the water to make a thin, pourable sauce. Crush the garlic to a paste with a little coarse sea salt. Add to the mayonnaise with the Parmesan and stir well. Thin it with a little more water, if necessary, so that the sauce remains pourable. Add pepper to taste and set aside.
2 Tear the lettuce leaves into large pieces and place in a large shallow salad bowl. Snip the anchovies into small pieces and scatter over the lettuce.
3 To make the croûtons, cut the bread into 3 cm (1¼ inch) slices. Cut off the crusts and discard. Dip a pastry brush into the melted butter and butter the slices of bread on all sides. Cut the bread into 3 cm (1¼ inch) cubes. Brush a large baking sheet with a little of the butter. Arrange the bread cubes on it in a single layer, brushing the cut sides with any remaining butter. Bake in a preheated oven, 200°C (400°F), Gas Mark 6, for about 12 minutes, or until crisp and a deep golden colour. Watch the croûtons carefully after 8 minutes, as they tend to colour quickly towards the end of the cooking time.
4 To serve, tip the hot croûtons into the salad and quickly drizzle the dressing over the top. Sprinkle the Parmesan over and serve at once.

Serves 4-6
Preparation time: 20 minutes
Cooking time: about 12 minutes
Oven temperature: 200°C (400°F), Gas Mark 6

Mayonnaise

2 egg yolks
1 tablespoon white wine vinegar or tarragon vinegar
1 teaspoon Dijon mustard
300 ml/½ pint olive oil
salt and pepper

1 Put the egg yolks in a bowl with the vinegar and mustard. Add about ½ teaspoon salt and a generous grinding of black pepper. Beat well to make a smooth paste.
2 Gradually beat in the oil, adding it 1 drop at a time at first. When the mixture begins to thicken, pour in the oil in a thin steady stream, beating constantly until all the oil has been added and the mayonnaise is smooth and thick.
3 Alternatively, combine the egg yolks, vinegar, mustard, salt and pepper in a blender or food processor. Process briefly on medium speed, then slowly add the oil through the feeder tube, drop by drop at first, then in a thin steady stream until all the oil has been incorporated and the mayonnaise is smooth and thick. Scrape into a bowl and serve or use as indicated in recipes.

Makes about 325 ml (11 fl oz)
Preparation time: 10-15 minutes

Spinach and Goats' Cheese Salad

The warm herb dressing coats the leaves and melts the goats' cheese in this interesting salad.

175 g/6 oz young spinach leaves
2 oranges, peeled and segmented
175 g/6 oz goats' cheese, diced
5 tablespoons olive oil
50 g/2 oz hazelnuts, roughly chopped
1 garlic clove, crushed
juice of 1 large orange
1 bunch of watercress, leaves stripped from the stalks, very finely chopped
2 tablespoons chopped fresh mixed herbs (e.g. parsley, tarragon, mint, dill, basil)
salt and pepper

1 Combine the spinach leaves, orange segments and goats' cheese in a large salad bowl.
2 Heat the olive oil in a small frying pan, add the hazelnuts and garlic and cook for 1-2 minutes. Stir in the orange juice, watercress and herbs. Heat through, then quickly pour the hot dressing on to the spinach. orange and goats' cheese. Add salt and pepper to taste, toss well and serve immediately.

Serves 4
Preparation time: 15 minutes
Cooking time: about 2 minutes

Mixed Leaf Salad with Spiced Toasted Nuts

175-250 g/6-8 oz mixed salad leaves
(e.g. lollo rosso, lamb's lettuce, youg
spinach, frisé, rocket, red oakleaf)
small handful of chervil or dill sprigs
6 tablespoons Classic French Dressing
(see page 54) or Yogurt Dressing (see
page 38)

SPICED NUTS:
25 g/1 oz butter
50 g/2 oz blanched almonds
50 g/2 oz pecan nuts
2 tablespoons pine nuts
1 teaspoon Worcestershire sauce
1 teaspoon mild chilli powder
pinch of ground cumin
salt

1 For the spiced nuts, melt the butter in a pan, add the remaining ingredients, cook over a moderate heat for 1 minute. Tip into a baking tin and place under a preheated moderate grill. Cook, turning frequently, for 5-10 minutes, until the nuts are evenly toasted. Allow to cool.
2 Mix the salad leaves and herbs in a large salad bowl. Spoon over the dressing, toss to coat the leaves, then scatter the spiced nuts over the top.

Serves 4-6
Preparation time: 10 minutes
Cooking time: 6-10 minutes

Summer Garden Salad with Croûtons

Edible flowers and summer herbs give this leafy salad an abundance of colour, while croûtons add extra crunch. For a special touch, cut the croûtons into pretty shapes, adding them to the salad at the last minute so they stay crisp.

175 g/6 oz mixed salad leaves (e.g. lamb's lettuce, frisé, nasturtium, chicory, oakleaf, watercress, radicchio, rocket, salad burnet)
handful of fresh herb sprigs (e.g. chervil, dill, fennel, chives)
40 g/1½ oz edible flowers (e.g. marigolds, dill or chive flowers, nasturtiums, pansies, pinks, borage)

1 quantity Classic French Dressing (see page 54)

GARLIC CROÛTONS:
1-2 garlic cloves
1 teaspoon salt
2 tablespoons olive oil
3 thick slices of white bread, crusts removed, cut into cubes or other shapes

1 Arrange a selection of salad leaves, herb sprigs and edible flowers in a large salad bowl.
2 To make the garlic croûtons, crush the garlic with the salt. Heat the olive oil in a frying pan. Add the bread cubes and fry for a few seconds, stirring constantly until they are beginning to brown. Stir in the garlic and continue cooking and stirring until the croûtons are golden brown and crisp. Drain on kitchen paper.
3 Pour the dressing over the salad and toss lightly. Sprinkle the croûtons on top of the salad.

Serves 4-6
Preparation time: 10 minutes
Cooking time: 3-4 minutes

VARIATIONS
Replace the French dressing with Walnut Dressing (see page 42) or Tarragon and Lemon Dressing (see right) if preferred.

Tarragon and Orange Dressing

This dressing is particularly good with fish, and would be delicious with smoked mackerel.

2 tablespoons tarragon vinegar
1 teaspoon finely grated orange rind
¼ teaspoon Dijon mustard
1 tablespoon chopped fresh tarragon
5 tablespoons olive oil or grapeseed oil
salt and pepper

1 Combine the vinegar, orange rind, mustard and tarragon in a small bowl. Add salt and pepper to taste. Stir to mix, then gradually whisk in the oil, using a balloon whisk.
2 Alternatively, mix all the ingredients in a screw-top jar, close the lid tightly and shake well to combine.

Makes about 75 ml/3 fl oz
Preparation time: 5 minutes

VARIATION

Tarragon and Lemon Dressing

Replace the orange rind with 1 teaspoon of finely grated lemon rind. Add a pinch of sugar.

White Cabbage and Red Onion Salad

500 g/1 lb white cabbage
2 small red onions, thinly sliced
2 dessert apples
1 tablespoon lemon juice
50 g/2 oz walnuts or pecan nuts,
    coarsely chopped
1 tablespoon poppy seeds (optional)
DRESSING:
5 tablespoons Mayonnaise (see
    page 15)
1 teaspoon Dijon or herb mustard
3 tablespoons yogurt or fromage frais
salt and pepper
or 1 quantity Horseradish and Soured
    Cream Dressing (see page 87)

1 Remove the core of the cabbage. Shred the rest finely and place in a large bowl with the onions.
2 Core and chop the apples and place in a small bowl with the lemon juice. Toss well to prevent them from discolouring, then add to the salad with the walnuts or pecans.
3 To make the dressing, mix the mayonnaise, mustard and yogurt or fromage frais together with salt and pepper to taste. Add to the salad and toss well. Serve sprinkled with poppy seeds, if liked.

Serves 6-8
Preparation time: 20 minutes

Frisé, Bacon and Hazelnut Salad

To serve this salad warm simply cut the bacon into strips, cook in a small frying pan until crisp, then add the dressing to the pan. Heat through gently before tossing the dressing and bacon with the frisé.

1 large head of frisé
5 rashers of rindless smoked streaky bacon
salt and pepper
1 quantity Hazelnut Dressing (see page 42)

1 Tear the frisé into large pieces and place in a salad bowl.
2 Grill the bacon on a rack under a preheated hot grill for 3-4 minutes, or until crisp, turning once or twice. Drain on kitchen paper, then use scissors to snip into small pieces. Add to the salad with salt and pepper to taste.
3 Pour the dressing over the salad and toss lightly.

Serves 4-6
Preparation time: 15 minutes
Cooking time: about 4 minutes

Chicory and Parmesan Salad

When arranged on individual plates this salad makes a wonderfully attractive starter; the chicory leaves can be used to scoop up the dressing and croûtons. Alternatively, the ingredients may be tossed casually together in a large bowl.

4 heads of chicory, trimmed, separated into leaves
50 g/2 oz piece of Parmesan cheese
DRESSING:
5 tablespoons Mayonnaise (see page 15) or Greek yogurt
1 tablespoon finely chopped fresh parsley (optional)
1 garlic clove, crushed

2 tablespoons finely grated Parmesan cheese
salt and pepper
CROUTONS:
3 thick slices of white bread, crusts removed
2 tablespoons light olive oil
25 g/1 oz butter

1 Start by making the dressing. Put the mayonnaise or Greek yogurt into a small bowl. Add the parsley, garlic and Parmesan. Stir in enough water to make a thin, pourable sauce. Season with salt and pepper and set aside.
2 To make the croûtons, cut the bread into small cubes. Heat the oil and butter in a frying pan until sizzling hot. Add the bread cubes and fry, stirring constantly, for 3-4 minutes, until the croûtons are golden and crisp. Drain on kitchen paper and sprinkle with salt to taste.
3 Arrange the chicory leaves on individual plates. Drizzle the dressing over the base of the leaves and pile the croûtons on top of the dressing. Using a cheese slicer or vegetable peeler, shave the Parmesan over the salad and serve garnished with parsley sprigs, if liked.

Serves 4
Preparation time: 20 minutes
Cooking time: about 3 minutes

Chicory and Pear Salad with Roquefort

2 large ripe pears
1 tablespoon lemon juice
1 orange, peeled and segmented
2 heads of chicory, separated into leaves
175 g/6 oz Roquefort cheese
2 tablespoons snipped chives
DRESSING:
3 tablespoons walnut oil
2 tablespoons white wine vinegar
½ teaspoon finely grated orange rind
pinch of sugar
salt and pepper

1 To make the dressing, stir all the ingredients together in a small bowl or mix in a screw-top jar, close the lid tightly and shake until combined.
2 Peel, core and thinly slice the pears and place in a small bowl with the lemon juice. Toss well to prevent them from discolouring. Arrange the pear slices, orange segments and chicory leaves on individual plates or in a shallow bowl. Pour the dressing over.
3 Just before serving, crumble the Roquefort over the salad and sprinkle with the chives.

Serves 4-6
Preparation time: 15 minutes

Radicchio and Orange Salad with Dates and Brie

Dates make a delicious addition to this combination of salad leaves, citrus fruit and Brie.

2 small oranges
1 head of radicchio, roughly torn
1 bunch of watercress or handful
 of rocket
250 g/8 oz fresh dates, stoned and
 chopped
175 g/6 oz Brie, rind removed, diced
6 tablespoons Sweet Mustard Dressing
 (see page 97) or Classic French
 Dressing (see page 54)
salt and coarsely ground black pepper

1 With a zester, remove small strips of rind from 1 of the oranges. Set aside. Using a small sharp knife, peel the rind and pith from both oranges. Slice them thinly.
2 Arrange all the salad ingredients in a serving bowl or on individual plates. Scatter the reserved orange rind over the top. Season with salt and coarsely ground black pepper. Drizzle the dressing over the salad just before serving.

Serves 4
Preparation time: 15 minutes

Oriental Cabbage Seaweed

A simple version of the deep-fried cabbage that masquerades as seaweed in many Chinese restaurants.

500 g/1 lb green cabbage, finely shredded
oil for deep-frying
pinch of caster sugar
salt
fine strips of red chilli, to garnish
CASHEW SALT:
50 g/2 oz salted roasted cashew nuts
¼ teaspoon Chinese seasoning

1 Start by making the cashew salt. Grind the cashew nuts finely in a liquidizer or food processor. Alternatively, put the cashew nuts between 2 sheets of greaseproof paper and crush with a rolling pin until quite fine. Stir in the Chinese seasoning and set aside.
2 Heat the oil for deep-frying to 180°-190°C (350-375°F), or until a cube of bread browns in 30 seconds. Add the shredded cabbage to the pan in small batches, and fry for about 1 minute per batch, until the cabbage is crisp. Drain well on kitchen paper and transfer to a shallow serving dish. Add a little sugar and salt, to taste.

3 Sprinkle the cashew salt over the cabbage and garnish with fine strips of red chilli. Serve at once.

Serves 4
Preparation time: 10 minutes
Cooking time: about 1 minute per batch

Continental Mixed Salad

A bright mixture of leaves and herbs is given a tangy sweetness with a raspberry dressing. When fresh raspberries are out of season, use homemade or ready-prepared raspberry vinegar for the vinaigrette.

1 red oakleaf lettuce, separated into
  leaves
½ head of frisé, separated into leaves
about 50 g/2 oz rocket
about 50 g/2 oz lamb's lettuce
small handful of fresh herb sprigs (e.g.
  chervil, dill, chives, basil, tarragon)
1 red onion, thinly sliced
1 large ripe avocado
1 tablespoon lemon juice

25 g/1 oz pine nuts, toasted
small handful of edible flowers (e.g.
  marigolds, nasturtiums, pansies –
  optional)
1 quantity Raspberry Vinaigrette (see
  right) or 1 quantity Classic French
  Dressing (see page 54)
salt and pepper

1 Tear the oakleaf lettuce leaves and the frisé into bite-sized pieces. Put in a large salad bowl with the rocket, lamb's lettuce, herbs and red onion.
2 Peel, halve and stone the avocado. Roughly chop the flesh and place in a small bowl with the lemon juice. Toss gently to prevent discoloration.
3 Just before serving, add the avocado, pine nuts and edible flowers to the salad, with salt and pepper to taste. Spoon the chosen dressing over and toss gently to mix.

Serves 4-6
Preparation time: 15 minutes

Fresh Raspberry Vinaigrette

125 g/4 oz fresh raspberries, hulled
1 teaspoon soft light brown sugar
2 tablespoons red wine vinegar
½ teaspoon Dijon mustard
½ garlic clove, crushed (optional)
5 tablespoons olive oil
salt and pepper

1 Combine the raspberries, sugar, vinegar, mustard and garlic, if using, in a small bowl. Mash with a fork until the raspberries are pulpy.
2 Using a wooden spoon, press the raspberry mixture through a sieve into a clean bowl. Whisk in the oil and add salt and pepper to taste.

Makes about 250 ml/8 fl oz
Preparation time: 10 minutes

VARIATION

Minted Raspberry Vinaigrette

Add 1 tablespoon of finely chopped mint to the sieved raspberry mixture before whisking in the oil.

Red Leaf Salad with Pecan Cheese Balls

175 g/6 oz mixed red salad leaves
　(e.g. red chicory, lollo rosso,
　red oakleaf, radicchio)
small handful of nasturtiums, pansies or
　other edible flowers
½ red onion, thinly sliced
1 quantity Yogurt Dressing (see
　page 38) or Sweet Mustard Dressing
　(see page 97)
CHEESE BALLS:
250 g/8 oz medium-soft goats' cheese
　(without rind) or cream cheese
40 g/1½ oz pecan nuts, very finely
　chopped
2 tablespoons paprika

1 Start by making the cheese balls.
Mix the cheese and pecan nuts in a
small bowl. Shape into about 16
small balls. Spread out the paprika
on a sheet of foil and lightly roll the
cheese balls in it to coat. Place on a
baking sheet and chill for at least
20 minutes or until required.
2 Arrange all the salad leaves and
flowers in a shallow serving bowl.
Add the onion and spoon the
dressing over. Add the cheese balls
and serve at once.

Serves 4
Preparation time: 20 minutes, plus
chilling time

Bitter Leaf Salad with Toasted Nuts and Seeds

As an alternative to the Yogurt Dressing in this salad, try Sweet Mustard Dressing (see page 97) to contrast with the bitter salad leaves.

25 g/1 oz flaked almonds
25 g/1 oz pine nuts
2 tablespoons sunflower seeds
1 small head of radicchio, separated into leaves
1 small head of frisé, separated into leaves
1 head of chicory, separated into leaves
1 mild onion, thinly sliced
1 quantity Yogurt Dressing (see page 38)
salt and pepper

1 Spread out all of the nuts and seeds in a single layer on a large baking sheet. Place under a preheated moderately hot grill and toast the nuts and seeds for 2-3 minutes, turning frequently until lightly browned. Transfer the mixture to a plate and leave to cool.
2 Tear the radicchio and frisé leaves into bite-sized pieces and place in a large salad bowl. Add the chicory and the onion, with salt and pepper to taste. Toss the salad leaves together lightly to mix evenly.
3 Spoon the dressing over the leaves and sprinkle the salad with the toasted nuts and seeds.

Serves 6
Preparation time: 10 minutes
Cooking time: 2-3 minutes

Warm Chorizo Salad

*Bitter salad leaves such as radicchio and chicory lend themselves
beautifully to warm salads. They are robust enough not to wilt as soon
as the dressing is added, and the action of the heat on the leaves
mellows their flavours wonderfully.*

about 250 g/8 oz salad leaves (e.g. radicchio, chicory, frisé)
small handful of sage leaves
5 tablespoons extra-virgin olive oil
300 g/10 oz chorizo sausage, skinned and thinly sliced
1 small red onion, thinly sliced
1 garlic clove, chopped
2 tablespoons red wine vinegar
salt and pepper

1 Arrange the salad leaves on individual plates, or tear the leaves into bite-sized pieces and place in a large salad bowl. Scatter over the sage leaves.
2 Heat the olive oil in a frying pan until fairly hot. Add the sliced chorizo sausage and fry over a high heat for 1 minute. Add the onion and garlic and fry for 1-2 minutes more, or until the chorizo is browned. Remove the pan from the heat.
3 Stir the vinegar into the pan, with salt and pepper to taste. Quickly spoon the mixture over the salad leaves and toss lightly. Serve at once.

Serves 4
Preparation time: 15 minutes
Cooking time: 2-3 minutes

Warm Duck and Orange Salad

This salad serves four as a starter; to have it as a main course, add another duck breast or two, and more salad leaves.

2 boneless duck breasts
1 tablespoon olive oil
2 teaspoons sesame oil
2 courgettes, sliced
1 garlic clove, chopped (optional)
2 small oranges, peeled and segmented
about 250 g/8 oz salad leaves (e.g.
   chicory, rocket, spinach, lollo rosso)
salt and pepper
DRESSING:
4 tablespoons olive oil
1 teaspoon sesame oil
1 tablespoon red wine vinegar
1 teaspoon grated orange rind
1 teaspoon finely chopped fresh parsley
pinch of dried sage
TO GARNISH:
toasted sesame seeds
long strips of orange rind

1 Using a sharp knife, make 4 diagonal slashes in the skin of each duck breast. Season with salt and pepper, rubbing the mixture into the skin and flesh.
2 Heat both the oils in a large frying pan. Add the duck breasts and cook over a fairly high heat for 5-7 minutes, turning once, until well browned on the outside but still rosy pink on the inside. Using tongs, transfer the duck breasts to a plate and keep warm.
3 Add the courgettes to the oil remaining in the pan, and stir in the garlic, if using. Cook, stirring, for 1-2 minutes, until the courgettes have started to soften. Using a slotted spoon, transfer to a bowl. Add the orange segments to the courgettes.
4 To make the dressing, stir all the ingredients together in a small bowl or place them in a screw-top jar, and shake well to combine.

5 Arrange the salad leaves on individual plates. Slice the duck breasts and arrange the slices next to the leaves, with portions of the courgette and orange salad next to the duck. Spoon the dressing over the salad and serve warm, garnished with a sprinkling of toasted sesame seeds and strips of orange rind.

Serves 4
Preparation time: 20 minutes
Cooking time: 6-9 minutes

Curried Chicken Salad

This salad is a superb variation on the well-known dish, Coronation Chicken. The chicken is mildly spiced and fruity. Fresh grapes are added and the salad is served on mixed leaves, which I find more appetizing than cold rice.

1 small whole cooked chicken, about 1.25 kg (2½ lb)
175 g/6 oz seedless grapes, halved
about 250 g/8 oz mixed salad leaves (e.g. cos, red oakleaf, lamb's lettuce, rocket, frisé)
salt and pepper
sprigs of fresh coriander, to garnish
DRESSING:
6 tablespoons Mayonnaise (see page 15)
1 tablespoon medium-hot curry paste
1-2 tablespoons mango chutney

1 Skin the chicken and remove all the meat from the carcass. Shred the meat into bite-sized pieces and place in a bowl with the grapes. Add salt and pepper to taste.

2 Tear the salad leaves into bite-sized pieces and arrange to form a bed on a serving platter or on individual plates.

3 Mix all the dressing ingredients together in a small bowl, adding just enough cold water to give a thick pouring consistency.

4 Add the dressing to the chicken mixture and toss gently until combined. Pile the mixture on to the salad leaves and garnish with a few sprigs of coriander.

Serves 4
Preparation time: 20 minutes

Gado Gado with Chicken

My favourite version of this Indonesian salad has shredded cooked chicken added together with all the vegetables, but vegetarians can easily omit the chicken or replace it with cubed tofu fried in a little oil until golden.

250 g/8 oz carrots, cut into matchsticks
175 g/6 oz celery, cut into matchsticks
175 g/6 oz leek, cut into matchsticks
125 g/4 oz mangetout
½ cucumber, peeled and cut in half lengthways
175 g/6 oz bean sprouts
about 175 g/6 oz pak choi

2 cooked chicken breasts, skinned and shredded
1 quantity Spicy Peanut Dressing (see right)
salt and pepper
chopped fresh coriander, to garnish (optional)

1 Bring a saucepan of water to the boil, add the carrot, celery and leek matchsticks to the boiling water and blanch for 1-2 minutes. Drain in a colander, refresh under cold running water, then drain again thoroughly. Tip into a large bowl.
2 Cut the mangetout in half diagonally. Using a teaspoon, scoop out the seeds from the cucumber and cut the flesh into slices.
3 Add the mangetout, cucumber and bean sprouts to the bowl. Season with salt and pepper. Gently toss all the vegetables together to mix.
4 Arrange the pak choi leaves on a serving platter or individual plates, with the shredded chicken and the vegetable mixture. Spoon the dressing over. Garnish with a sprinkling of chopped coriander if liked.

Serves 4
Preparation time: 30 minutes
Cooking time: 1-2 minutes

Spicy Peanut Dressing

Make this rich spicy dressing a little in advance to allow the flavours to develop before using. It is the perfect dressing for the Indonesian vegetable salad, Gado Gado, but is also delicious with grilled chicken, fish or shellfish.

25 g/1 oz creamed coconut
4 tablespoons milk
½ small onion, chopped
1 garlic clove, crushed
4 tablespoons smooth peanut butter
1 teaspoon soft light brown sugar
2 teaspoons soy sauce
½ teaspoon ground cumin
½ teaspoon chilli powder
salt and pepper

1 Chop the creamed coconut and place in a small pan with the milk. Heat gently for about 2 minutes, stirring, until the coconut melts and forms a paste with the milk.
2 Transfer the coconut mixture to a liquidizer or food processor. Add all the remaining ingredients, purée until smooth, then scrape into a small bowl. Cover and set aside until required.

Makes about 175 ml/6 fl oz
Preparation time: 10 minutes
Cooking time: 2 minutes

Hot Chicken and Walnut Salad

Celebrate a summer evening with this hot salad.

125 g/4 oz mangetout, halved
about 250 g/8 oz mixed salad leaves
   (e.g. red oakleaf, batavia, frisé,
   radicchio)
½ red onion, thinly sliced
3 skinless chicken breast fillets
3 tablespoons light olive oil
3 tablespoons walnut oil
1 garlic clove, crushed
2 tablespoons sherry vinegar or wine
   vinegar
50 g/2 oz walnut pieces
rind of 1 lemon, cut into thin strips
1 teaspoon soft light brown sugar
salt and coarsely ground black pepper
handful of parsley sprigs, torn,
   to garnish (optional)

1 Bring a saucepan of water to the boil, add the mangetout and blanch for 1 minute. Drain in a colander, refresh under cold running water, then drain again thoroughly.
2 Tear the salad leaves into bite-sized pieces. Arrange with the mangetout and the onion around the edge of a large serving platter or individual plates.
3 Cut the chicken breasts into thick slices and, using a rolling pin, flatten the slices between 2 sheets of greaseproof paper or clingfilm to give thin 'medallions'.

4 Heat the olive oil in a large frying pan. Add the chicken pieces, a few at a time, and cook over a high heat for about 2 minutes, turning once, until lightly browned and cooked through. Using tongs, transfer the 'medallions' to a plate and keep warm while cooking the remaining chicken pieces.
5 Add the walnut oil to the oil remaining in the pan. Stir in the remaining ingredients, with salt and pepper to taste. Heat through,

stirring, then return the chicken to the pan. Toss the chicken pieces in the hot dressing to coat.
6 Pile the hot chicken mixture in the centre of the salad leaves. Serve at once, scattered with torn parsley leaves, if liked.

Serves 4
Preparation time: 30 minutes
Cooking time: about 12 minutes

Chef's Salad

A chef's salad can contain almost any combination of ingredients – it's really a way of using up whatever is in the refrigerator! This version has chicken, smoked ham and cheese, but you may want to include other ingredients.

1 small lettuce (e.g. round, red oakleaf, batavia, frisé), separated into leaves
small handful of mixed herb sprigs
¼ cucumber, thinly sliced
25 g/1 oz walnut pieces
about 250 g/8 oz cooked chicken, diced
125 g/4 oz smoked ham, cut into strips
75 g/3 oz cheese (e.g. Edam, Emmental or mature Cheddar), crumbled
handful of seedless grapes, halved (optional)
salt and pepper
1 quantity Classic French Dressing (see page 54) or Blue Cheese Dressing (see below)

1 Tear the lettuce into bite-sized pieces and place in a large salad bowl with the herb sprigs. Toss together lightly.
2 Add all the remaining ingredients except the dressing, with salt and pepper to taste.
3 Just before serving, spoon over the dressing and toss lightly.

Serves 4
Preparation time: 20 minutes

Blue Cheese Dressing

175 g/ 6 oz dolcelatte or other full-flavoured, creamy blue cheese
1 shallot, very finely chopped
125 ml/4 fl oz fromage frais
5 tablespoons milk
salt and pepper

1 Place the dolcelatte in a bowl and mash with a fork to break it up. Add the shallot and mix well.
2 Add the fromage frais to the blue cheese mixture and mash with the fork to make a paste. Stir in the milk and add salt and pepper to taste.

Makes about 350 ml/12 fl oz
Preparation time: 10 minutes

Smoked Chicken and Citrus Salad

Refreshing chunks of grapefruit and orange are tossed with smoked chicken in this summery salad. Pink peppercorns are a colourful touch, but some people are allergic to them.

375 g/12 oz smoked chicken,
  off the bone
1 pink grapefruit
2 small oranges
½ cucumber, thinly sliced
1 small fennel bulb, trimmed and
  thinly sliced (optional)
1 round lettuce, separated into leaves

about 50 g/2 oz frisé
about 50 g/2 oz lamb's lettuce or
  watercress
pink peppercorns (optional)
1 quantity Yogurt Dressing (see right)
  or Tarragon and Orange Dressing
  (see page 18)
salt and pepper

1 Skin the smoked chicken and cut the flesh into bite-sized pieces. Place in a large bowl.
2 Using a small sharp knife, peel the grapefruit and oranges, taking care to remove all the pith. Working over a bowl to catch the juices, segment and roughly chop the flesh. Set the juice aside. Add the citrus fruit to the chicken with the cucumber and fennel, if liked. Toss lightly.
3 Arrange the chicken mixture and the salad leaves on individual plates.
4 To serve, stir the reserved citrus juices and the pink peppercorns, if liked, into the dressing, and pour it over the salad.

Serves 4
Preparation time: 30 minutes

Yogurt Dressing

*Low in fat and calories, this dressing can be varied to taste by adding chopped herbs or pickles, garlic, curry paste or finely grated orange rind.
I prefer to use live yogurt, which has a mild creamy flavour, but any natural yogurt will do.*

150 ml (¼ pint) natural yogurt
1 tablespoon lemon juice
1 teaspoon clear honey
½ teaspoon Dijon mustard
salt and pepper

1 Beat all the ingredients together in a small bowl with a wooden spoon until smooth. Add salt and pepper to taste.

Makes about 175 ml/6 fl oz
Preparation time: 2 minutes

Pesto Chicken and Pepper Salad

1 small cooked chicken
1 red pepper
1 yellow pepper
50 g/2 oz black olives
about 75 g/3 oz mixed salad leaves
   (e.g. rocket, frisé, young spinach)
1 quantity Pesto Dressing (see right)
salt and pepper
sprigs of basil, to garnish

1 Skin the chicken and remove all the meat from the carcass. Shred the meat and set aside.
2 Cook the peppers under a preheated hot grill for 15-20 minutes, turning occasionally, until the skin is blistered and blackened all over. Transfer the peppers to a bowl, cover with several layers of kitchen paper and set aside.
3 When cool enough to handle, rub off and discard the charred skin from the peppers. Slice the flesh into thin rings, discarding the seeds. Season with salt and pepper.
4 Arrange the salad leaves on a serving dish or individual plates. Pile the peppers on to the salad leaves, with the olives and chicken. Pour the dressing over the chicken mixture and toss lightly. Serve at once, garnished with sprigs of basil.

Serves 4
Preparation time: 20 minutes
Cooking time: 20 minutes

Pesto Dressing

25 g/1 oz basil leaves
25 g/1 oz Parmesan cheese, grated
1 tablespoon pine nuts
4 tablespoons white wine vinegar
1 garlic clove, crushed
pepper
125 ml/4 fl oz extra-virgin olive oil

1 Combine the basil leaves, Parmesan, pine nuts, vinegar and garlic in a liquidizer or food processor. Add pepper to taste. Process for a few seconds.

2 With the blender or food processor running, drizzle in the olive oil through the feeder tube until the mixture becomes thick and smooth. Pour into a bowl or jug and use as required.

Makes about 250 ml/8 fl oz
Preparation time: 5 minutes

Rare Beef Salad

1 red pepper, halved, cored
   and deseeded
375 g/12 oz beef fillet, cut into
   2.5 cm/1 inch steaks
500 g/1 lb small new potatoes,
   scrubbed
125 g/4 oz French beans, topped and
   tailed
½ red onion, thinly sliced
125 g/4 oz red and yellow cherry
   tomatoes, halved
about 16 green olives, preferably
   anchovy-stuffed
few black olives (optional)
2 teaspoons chopped fresh thyme
1 quantity Sweet Mustard Dressing (see
   page 97)
salt and coarsely ground black pepper

1 Cook the pepper halves skin side up under a preheated hot grill for 10-15 minutes, without turning, until the skin is blistered and blackened all over. Transfer to a bowl, cover with kitchen paper and set aside.
2 Season the beef liberally with pepper. Grill for about 5 minutes, turning once, until well browned on the outside but still rare inside. Transfer to a plate and leave to cool.
3 Rub off and discard the charred skin from the pepper halves and cut the flesh into strips. Set aside.
4 Bring a large saucepan of water to the boil, add the potatoes and cook for 10-12 minutes, or until just tender. Drain in a colander, cool under cold running water, then drain again thoroughly.

5 Bring a second saucepan of water to the boil, add the French beans and blanch for 1-2 minutes. Drain in a colander, refresh under cold running water, then drain thoroughly.
6 Cut the potatoes in half. Place in a bowl with the pepper strips, French beans, onion, tomatoes and olives. Slice the beef thinly, cutting across the grain, and add to the bowl with the thyme. Add salt and pepper to taste.
7 Spoon the dressing over the salad and toss lightly to mix.

Serves 4-6
Preparation time: 30 minutes
Cooking time: about 25 minutes

Crisp Duck and Red Fruit Salad

Fruits and duck always go well together – the fresh juiciness of the fruit contrasts with the rich flavour of the bird. You can simplify the salad by using only one fruit or you could be extravagant and extend the selection.

2.5 kg/5 lb oven-ready duckling
about 250 g/8 oz salad leaves (e.g.
    red oakleaf, lamb's lettuce, rocket,
    cos, batavia, four seasons)
175 g/6 oz red cherries
75 g/3 oz raspberries, hulled
75 g/3 oz redcurrants

1 box mustard and cress (optional)
2 tablespoons snipped fresh chives
1 quantity Classic French Dressing (see
    page 54) or Walnut Dressing
    (see right)
salt and coarsely ground black pepper

1 Wash the duckling and pat dry. Prick the flesh all over with a fork. Rub the skin with salt and pepper and place the bird on a rack set over a roasting tin. Roast in a preheated oven, 180°C (350°F), Gas Mark 4, for 2½ hours. Leave to cool.
2 Strip the skin from the duck and place it on a grill rack. Cook under a preheated hot grill until crisp, then leave to cool.
3 Remove the meat from the duck and shred or cut it into bite-sized pieces. Using kitchen scissors, snip the crisped duck skin into small pieces.
4 Arrange the salad leaves and fruits on a serving platter or individual plates. Sprinkle over the mustard and cress, if liked, and the chives. Arrange the pieces of duck on the salad and scatter over the crisped duck skin. Add salt and pepper to taste.
5 Spoon the chosen dressing over the salad and serve at once.

Serves 4-6
Preparation time: 35 minutes
Cooking time: 2¾ hours

Walnut Dressing

Nut dressings like this one add interest to pasta or rice salads and are also excellent with mixed salads.

3 tablespoons balsamic vinegar or
    sherry vinegar
1 teaspoon soft light brown sugar
1 teaspoon Dijon mustard
125 ml/4 fl oz walnut oil
1 tablespoon finely chopped walnuts
1 tablespoon chopped fresh parsley or
    other herb (sage, thyme or basil)
salt and pepper

1 Combine the vinegar, sugar and mustard in a small bowl. Add salt and pepper to taste. Stir to mix, then gradually whisk in the walnut oil, using a balloon whisk.
2 Stir the chopped walnuts and herbs into the dressing and adjust the seasoning to taste.

Makes about 150 ml/¼ pint
Preparation time: 10 minutes

VARIATION

Hazelnut Dressing

Replace the walnut oil and chopped walnuts with hazelnut oil and chopped hazelnuts.

Hot Chicken Liver Salad

25 g/1 oz butter
5 tablespoons light olive oil
500 g/1 lb chicken livers, halved
2 tablespoons red wine vinegar
1 teaspoon wholegrain mustard
about 250 g/8 oz mixed salad leaves
   (e.g. red oakleaf, frisé, radicchio,
   chicory)
2 spring onions, thinly sliced
Sprigs of flat leaf parsley
salt and pepper

1 Heat the butter and the oil in a large frying pan. Add the chicken livers and cook over a high heat for 3-4 minutes, stirring frequently, until sealed and browned on the outside but still lightly pink within. Remove from the heat and stir in the vinegar and mustard, with salt and pepper to taste.
2 Arrange the salad leaves on individual serving plates.
3 Spoon the hot chicken liver mixture on top of the salad leaves and sprinkle with the spring onions and sprigs of parsley. Serve at once.

Serves 4
Preparation time: 20 minutes
Cooking time: 3-4 minutes

Mixed Deli Platter

When even small corner shops have a well-stocked delicatessen counter, it is a matter of moments to create this appetizing platter.

1 red pepper, halved, cored and
   deseeded
1 yellow pepper, halved, cored and
   deseeded
3 small pickled gherkins, chopped
2 spring onions, shredded
2 tablespoons olive oil
1 teaspoon lemon juice
375-500 g/12-16 oz cold cooked
   meats, sliced (e.g. salami, pastrami,
   ham, sausage, turkey, corned beef)
salt and pepper
radishes and black olives,
   to garnish (optional)

1 Place the pepper halves skin side up on a grill rack. Cook under a preheated hot grill, without turning, for 10-15 minutes or until the skin is blistered and blackened all over. Transfer to a bowl, cover with several layers of kitchen paper and set aside.
2 When the peppers are cool enough to handle, rub off and discard the charred skin. Roughly chop the flesh and place in a bowl.
3 Add the chopped pickled gherkins and spring onions to the bowl. Pour over the olive oil and lemon juice and add salt and pepper to taste. Toss well.

4 Just before serving, arrange the sliced meats around the edge of a large serving platter or divide between individual plates. Spoon the pepper and gherkin mixture into the centre. Garnish with radishes and olives, if liked.

Serves 4-6
Preparation time: 10 minutes
Cooking time: 10-15 minutes

FISH AND SEAFOOD

Crab Salad

To save time you can buy ready-dressed crab meat, but I like to prepare my own and think it gives a far better result.

1 large cooked crab, about 1 kg/2 lb
1-2 tablespoons lemon juice
3-4 tablespoons Mayonnaise (see page 15)
about 250 g/8 oz mixed salad leaves (e.g. frisé, red oakleaf, lollo rosso, batavia,
lamb's lettuce, rocket, chicory)
handful of fresh herb sprigs (e.g. chervil, dill, parsley, coriander)
3 spring onions, finely shredded
½ cucumber, peeled and finely diced
salt and pepper
lemon wedges, to garnish

1 Remove the large claws and legs from the crab. Crack open with a rolling pin or small hammer and remove the white flesh. Flake into a bowl.

2 Prise open the body of the crab. Remove any white meat and add to the bowl. Carefully remove all of the brown meat from the body and shell, discarding the inedible mouth parts, the grey stomach sac and the feathery-looking gills or 'dead men's fingers'. Add the brown meat to the bowl.

3 Add the lemon juice and mayonnaise to the crab, adjusting the quantities according to taste and seasoning with salt and pepper. Mix thoroughly.

4 Just before serving, arrange the salad leaves on a serving platter or on individual plates. Scatter over the herb sprigs, the spring onion shreds and the diced cucumber.

5 Pile the crab meat on to the platter or plates. Serve at once, garnished with lemon wedges.

Serves 4
Preparation time: 30 minutes

Dressed Lobster

Because lobsters are expensive, I think it is best to serve them as simply as possible, without masking their sea-fresh, slightly sweet flavour and luxurious texture with a great many other ingredients or rich, buttery or creamy sauces.

2 cooked lobsters, about 1 kg/2 lb each, or 4 smaller lobsters
1 quantity Mayonnaise (see page 15)
1 teaspoon finely grated lemon rind
3 tablespoons lemon juice
salt and pepper
pinch of cayenne pepper (optional)

TO GARNISH:
lemon slices
few salad leaves

1 Split the lobsters in half lengthways down the centre. Pull out the intestinal vein that runs from the head to the tail and remove and discard any grey gills or 'fingers'. Thoroughly clean out the head cavity.
2 Crack the claws with a rolling pin or small hammer and carefully remove the flesh. Remove the body meat and cut into thick slices. Rinse the shells, pat them dry with kitchen paper and set them aside.
3 Mix the mayonnaise, lemon rind and juice in a bowl. Spoon the mixture into the head cavities of the shells. Pile the body meat back into the shells. Season with salt, pepper and a little cayenne, if liked.
4 To serve, arrange the dressed lobsters with their claw meat on individual plates. If using large lobsters, allow ½ a lobster per serving; alternatively, allow 1 small whole lobster each. Garnish each portion with lemon slices and a few salad leaves.

Serves 4
Preparation time: 40 minutes

Tuna and Coriander Salad

French beans, lightly cooked to retain their crispness, make the base for this salad, as a change from mixed leaves.

250 g/8 oz French beans, topped and tailed
2 x 200 g/7 oz cans tuna in brine, drained
½ red onion, thinly sliced
1 teaspoon finely grated lemon rind
handful of fresh coriander leaves, roughly torn
1 quantity Classic French Dressing (see page 54)
salt and pepper
lemon wedges, to garnish

1 Bring a saucepan of water to the boil. Add the French beans. Cook for 2 minutes, then drain. Refresh under cold water, then drain well.
2 Flake the tuna and place it in a large bowl. Add the onion, lemon rind and coriander with salt and pepper to taste. Pour the dressing over and toss gently.
3 To serve, arrange a bed of cooked French beans on a serving platter or on individual plates. Pile the tuna and coriander mixture on top and garnish with lemon wedges.

Serves 4
Preparation time: 20 minutes
Cooking time: 2 minutes

Mussel Salad with Bacon and Tomato Vinaigrette

1 kg/2 lb mussels
2 shallots, finely chopped
6 tablespoons dry white wine
  or water
6 rashers of rindless smoked
  streaky bacon
50 g/2 oz piece of Parmesan cheese
sprigs of fresh basil or parsley,
  to garnish (optional)

DRESSING:

6 tablespoons tomato juice
4 tablespoons extra-virgin olive oil
2 tablespoons red wine vinegar
½ garlic clove, crushed
¼ teaspoon caster sugar
1 tablespoon finely shredded fresh
  basil
salt and pepper

1 Start by making the dressing. Whisk all the ingredients together in a small bowl or place in a screw-top jar, close the lid tightly and shake until combined. Set aside.

2 Discard any mussels that do not close when tapped firmly. Scrub to clean thoroughly and remove the 'beards'. Place the mussels in a large saucepan with the shallots and white wine or water, cover and cook over a high heat for 3-4 minutes, or until most of the shells have opened. Drain, discarding the cooking liquid and any unopened mussels. Transfer the mussels and shallots to a serving bowl and leave to cool. Remove some of the shells, if you like, for ease of eating.

3 Meanwhile, cook the bacon under a preheated hot grill until crisp. Drain on kitchen paper. Crumble or snip into small pieces.

4 Pour the dressing over the mussel mixture, toss lightly, then scatter the bacon over the top. Adjust the seasoning to taste. Using a potato peeler, 'shave' the Parmesan over the top. Serve the salad scattered with fresh basil or parsley, if liked.

Serves 4
Preparation time: 25 minutes
Cooking time: 8-9 minutes

Mussels with Croûtons and Tomato Vinaigrette

Non-meat-eaters can also enjoy the salad by omitting the bacon and replacing it with these large, crusty croûtons.

50 g/2 oz butter, softened
2 garlic cloves, crushed
4 thick slices white bread
salt

1 Preheat the oven to 200°C (400°F), Gas Mark 6. In a small bowl mix together the butter and garlic. Spread the bread slices with the garlic butter and then cut into squares. Arrange in a single layer on a baking sheet and bake in the oven for 8-10 minutes, until crisp and golden. Sprinkle with salt. Add the croûtons to the mussels just before serving so they remain crisp.

Butterfly Prawns with Basil

500 g/1 lb uncooked king prawns in
  their shells
about 175 g/6 oz salad leaves (e.g.
  frisé, lamb's lettuce, rocket, batavia)
125 g/4 oz cherry tomatoes, halved
few sprigs of basil, leaves removed
  from stems and roughly torn
½ quantity Tarragon and Lemon
  Dressing (see page 18) or Garlic and
  Herb Mayonnaise (see page 95)

MARINADE:
3 tablespoons lemon juice
3 tablespoons light olive oil
½ garlic clove, crushed
1 tablespoon chopped fresh basil
salt and pepper

1 Remove the heads from the
prawns. Using sharp kitchen scissors,
carefully cut the prawns lengthways,
almost in half, leaving the tail end
intact. Place them in a single layer in
a shallow dish.
2 Mix all the marinade ingredients in
a small bowl. Pour over the prawns,
cover the dish and leave for 1 hour.
3 Arrange the prawns in a single
layer on a rack over a grill pan.
Place under a preheated hot grill
and cook for 3-4 minutes, until the
prawns have curled or 'butterflied'
and are bright pink in colour.
4 Meanwhile, arrange the salad
leaves and tomatoes on a serving
platter or individual plates. Scatter
the basil leaves over.

5 Arrange the hot butterfly prawns on
the salad. Serve at once, with the
dressing or mayonnaise.

Serves 2-4
Preparation time: 30 minutes, plus
1 hour marinating time
Cooking time: 3-4 minutes

Smoked Salmon and Quails' Egg Salad

Quails' eggs and smoked salmon make this a rather special salad. If you prefer you can substitute hens' eggs – use 4 eggs, poached for 5 minutes, or gently fried in butter until just set.

250 g/8 oz small new potatoes
about 250 g/8 oz mixed salad leaves
(e.g. frisé, rocket, lamb's lettuce,
escarole, salad burnet)
2-3 tablespoons croûtons (see Chicory
and Parmesan Salad, page 23)
1 teaspoon white wine vinegar
12 quails' eggs
125 g/4 oz smoked salmon, cut into
strips
2 tablespoons snipped chives
salt and pepper
DRESSING:
5 tablespoons Mayonnaise (see
page 15) or Garlic and Herb
Mayonnaise (see page 95)
1 tablespoon lemon juice
3-4 tablespoons water

1 Bring a saucepan of water to the boil, add the potatoes and cook for about 10 minutes, or until just tender. Drain in a colander and refresh under cold running water. Drain again thoroughly. Allow to cool completely, then cut the potatoes into halves or quarters.

2 To make the dressing, mix together the mayonnaise, lemon juice and measured water.
3 Shortly before serving, arrange the salad leaves in a large shallow serving dish or on individual plates. Scatter the croûtons over the top.
4 Bring a frying pan of water to simmering point. Add the vinegar. Carefully break in 6 of the eggs and poach for about 1 minute. Using a slotted spoon, transfer the poached

eggs to a plate and repeat with the rest of the eggs. Alternatively, fry the eggs in butter until just firm.
5 Arrange the cooked quails' eggs and salmon strips on the salad and scatter over the snipped chives. Add salt and pepper to taste. Drizzle over the dressing or serve separately.

Serves 4
Preparation time: 20 minutes
Cooking time: 12-15 minutes

Fried Scallop Salad

Tender scallops and stir-fried red pepper strips make for a sophisticated salad to serve as a first course.

8 large fresh scallops
3 tablespoons light olive oil
½ small red pepper, cored, deseeded
    and cut into matchstick strips
1 quantity Classic French Dressing
    (see right)

1 tablespoon chopped fresh parsley
125 g/4 oz rocket
½ small head frisé, leaves roughly torn
2 spring onions, finely shredded
salt and pepper

1 Remove the corals from the scallops and set aside. Trim the white parts and cut each in half horizontally. Using a sharp knife, lightly score each scallop piece in a lattice pattern.
2 Heat the oil in a large frying pan. Add the scallops, including the corals. Cook, stirring frequently, for 3-4 minutes, or until opaque. Using a slotted spoon, transfer the scallops to a plate.
3 Add the red pepper strips to the pan and cook, stirring, for 1 minute. Pour the dressing into the pan and heat through. Stir in the parsley, then remove the pan from the heat. Return the scallops to the pan and add salt and pepper to taste.
4 Arrange a bed of rocket and frisé on individual serving plates. Scatter over the shredded spring onions.
5 Spoon the warm scallop mixture on to the plates and serve at once.

Serves 4
Preparation time: 25 minutes
Cooking time: about 6 minutes

Classic French Dressing

This basic recipe for French Dressing can easily be adapted by adding ingredients such as chopped fresh herbs, grated onion, chopped anchovy fillets or capers or finely grated lemon or orange rind.

2 tablespoons red or white wine
    vinegar
1-2 garlic cloves, crushed
2 teaspoons Dijon mustard
¼ teaspoon caster sugar
6 tablespoons olive oil
salt and pepper

1 Combine the vinegar, garlic, mustard and sugar in a small bowl. Add salt and pepper and stir well.
2 Gradually whisk in the olive oil. Taste and add more salt and pepper if necessary.
3 Alternatively, put all the ingredients in a screw-top jar, close the lid tightly and shake well until combined. Use as required.

Makes about 150 ml/¼ pint
Preparation time: 5 minutes

Monkfish Salad with Coriander and Mint

Monkfish is an excellent salad ingredient, as it has firm flesh and very good flavour.

500 g/1 lb monkfish, filleted
1 x 400 g/14 oz can pimientos, drained
5 tablespoons olive oil
1 tablespoon coriander seeds, crushed
1 onion, sliced
2 garlic cloves, chopped
3 tablespoons capers, rinsed and drained
pared rind of ½ lemon, cut into thin matchstick strips
few sprigs of coriander, roughly torn
few sprigs of mint, leaves stripped from the stems and roughly torn
1 tablespoon balsamic vinegar or lemon juice
about 125 g/4 oz mixed salad leaves (e.g. cos, lamb's lettuce, rocket, frisé, lollo rosso), to serve (optional)
salt and pepper

1 Cut the monkfish fillet into thin slices and set aside.

2 Tip the canned pimientos into a colander. Rinse under cold running water, then drain well. Cut the pimientos into strips.

3 Heat the olive oil in a large frying pan. Add the coriander seeds and cook over a moderate heat for a few seconds. Add the onion, cook for about 5 minutes, stirring frequently until softened but not browned. Add the garlic, cook for 1 minute more.

4 Increase the heat to moderately high. Add the monkfish slices to the pan and cook, stirring gently, for 3-4 minutes, or until the fish is firm and opaque. Lower the heat and stir in the pimiento strips, capers and strips of lemon rind. Remove the pan from the heat and leave to cool for a few minutes.

5 Add the coriander and mint to the pan with the balsamic vinegar or lemon juice. Season to taste with salt and pepper and toss lightly. Serve the monkfish salad warm or allow to cool completely. If liked, arrange a bed of salad leaves on a serving platter or individual plates and spoon the monkfish mixture on top.

Serves 4
Preparation time: 15 minutes
Cooking time: about 10 minutes

Mixed Seafood Salad

You can make this salad very simply, using a ready prepared chilled or frozen seafood mixture sold in most supermarkets. Alternatively, you can go to town with the seafood and include such treats as crayfish tails, langoustine, crab claws, Mediterranean prawns and scallops. The exact weight you require will vary depending on whether the ingredients are shelled or not.

500-750 g/1-1½ lb mixed cooked
   seafood (e.g. prawns, crab claws,
   langoustines, scallops, mussels,
   squid)
1 lemon, cut into wedges
1 lime, cut into wedges
coarse sea salt
herb sprigs, to garnish
salad leaves, to serve (optional)
DRESSING:
2 tablespoons capers, rinsed and
   drained
8 tablespoons Mayonnaise (see
   page 15)
1 teaspoon finely chopped lemon rind
2 tablespoons chopped fresh dill
   or tarragon
salt and pepper

1 To make the dressing, put the capers in a small bowl and mash them with a fork to break them up. Add the mayonnaise, lemon rind and dill or tarragon, with salt and pepper to taste. Mix well.

2 Spoon a little of the dressing in the centre of a serving platter or individual plates. Arrange the seafood on the plates with the lemon and lime wedges. Sprinkle with sea salt, garnish with herbs and serve with salad leaves, if liked. Offer any remaining dressing separately.

Serves 4
Preparation time: 20 minutes

Courgette Salad with Lemon and Thyme

500 g/1 lb small courgettes
about 16 black olives
DRESSING:
5 tablespoons extra-virgin olive oil
pared rind of 1 lemon, cut into thin strips
125 ml/4 fl oz lemon juice
1 garlic clove, crushed
1 tablespoon roughly chopped fresh thyme
1 teaspoon clear honey
salt and pepper

1 Start by making the dressing. Whisk all the ingredients together in a small bowl or place in a screw-top jar, close the lid tightly and shake to combine.

2 Cut the courgettes in half crossways. Using a small sharp knife, cut both ends of each piece of courgette to a point, 'sharpening' it just as you would do a pencil.

3 Bring a saucepan of water to the boil, add the courgettes and cook for 2 minutes. Drain immediately, blot the excess moisture with kitchen paper and transfer to a serving bowl. Add the olives.

4 Pour the dressing over the warm courgettes, toss lightly and leave until cold before serving.

Serves 4-6
Preparation time: 20 minutes, plus standing time
Cooking time: 2 minutes

Grilled Pepper and Onion Salad

The smoky flavours of grilled peppers, onions and garlic contrast wonderfully well with balsamic vinegar dressing.

3 onions
3 red peppers
3 yellow peppers
15 garlic cloves
1½ tablespoons fennel seeds
6 tablespoons olive oil
2 tablespoons balsamic vinegar
3 tablespoons roughly chopped fresh parsley
salt and pepper

1 Cut the onions into wedges, keeping the root ends intact so that the layers do not separate. Bring a saucepan of water to the boil, add the onions and cook for 1 minute, then drain well.

2 Halve the peppers lengthways, cutting through the stems. Remove the seeds. Place the peppers, skin side up, in a grill pan. Add the onions and garlic cloves. Cook under a preheated hot grill for about 10-15 minutes, turning occasionally, until the pepper skins are blistered and blackened all over. Turn the onions and garlic as necessary but let them char too.

3 Transfer the peppers to a bowl, cover with several layers of kitchen paper and cool slightly. Rub off the charred skin. Arrange the peppers, onions and 12 of the garlic cloves on individual plates.

4 In a dry pan, toast the fennel seeds for a few minutes until they begin to pop and smell aromatic. Using a mortar and pestle, or a small strong bowl and the end of a rolling pin, roughly crush the fennel seeds with the 3 remaining grilled garlic cloves.

5 Whisk in the oil and vinegar, and season to taste.

6 Sprinkle the parsley over the salad and then spoon over the dressing. Serve this salad at room temperature.

Serves 6
Preparation time: 20 minutes
Cooking time: 11-16 minutes

Garden Salad

Cauliflower, peas and crisp rosy radishes with a creamy mint dressing – this salad is evocative of an English vegetable garden.

1 small cauliflower, broken into florets
175 g/6 oz podded fresh peas (about
    375 g/12 oz in the pods)
1 bunch radishes, trimmed
4 spring onions, chopped
2 tablespoons chopped fresh parsley
salt and pepper
sprigs of mint and flat leaf parsley,
    to garnish
DRESSING:
6 tablespoons Mayonnaise (see
    page 15)
3 tablespoons natural yogurt
3 tablespoons water
½ clove garlic, crushed (optional)
1-2 tablespoons finely chopped fresh
    mint

1 Bring a saucepan of water to the boil. Add the cauliflower florets. When the water returns to the boil, cook the florets for about 3 minutes, until just tender. Drain in a colander and refresh under cold running water, then drain thoroughly.
2 Add the peas to a saucepan of boiling water. Cook for 4 minutes then drain, refresh and cool as for the cauliflower.
3 Combine the cauliflower, peas, radishes and spring onions in a serving bowl. Add the parsley, with salt and pepper to taste.

4 To make the dressing, stir all the ingredients together in a small bowl. Adjust the seasoning to taste. Drizzle over the salad and toss lightly before serving, garnished with sprigs of mint and flat leaf parsley.

Serves 4-6
Preparation time: 25 minutes
Cooking time: about 7 minutes

Grilled Asparagus Salad

Choose asparagus spears of medium thickness for this salad. It is also delicious with a dressing of garlic mayonnaise thinned to a pouring consistency with a little water.

500 g/1 lb asparagus
3 tablespoons olive oil
about 50 g/2 oz rocket
about 50 g/2 oz lamb's lettuce
2 spring onions, finely chopped
3-4 radishes, thinly sliced

6 tablespoons Tarragon and Lemon
  Dressing (see page 18) or Classic
  French Dressing (see page 54)
salt and pepper
TO GARNISH:
roughly chopped fresh herbs (e.g.
  tarragon, parsley, chervil, dill)
thin strips of lemon rind

1 Trim the asparagus and use a potato peeler to peel about 5 cm (2 inches) off the base of each stalk. Arrange the asparagus in a single layer on a baking sheet and brush with olive oil. Cook under a preheated hot grill for about 7 minutes, turning frequently, until the asparagus spears are just tender when pierced with the point of a sharp knife and lightly patched with brown. Sprinkle with salt and pepper and leave to cool.
2 Arrange the rocket and lamb's lettuce on a serving platter or individual plates. Scatter over the spring onions and radishes.
3 Arrange the asparagus beside the salad leaves and drizzle with the dressing. Garnish with a sprinkling of roughly chopped fresh herbs and thin strips of lemon rind.

Serves 4
Preparation time: 15 minutes
Cooking time: about 7 minutes

Roasted Asparagus with Coriander and Lime

750 g/1½ lb asparagus spears
8 tablespoons olive oil
3 tablespoons freshly squeezed
  lime juice
coarse sea salt and coarsely ground
  black pepper
torn coriander leaves, to garnish

1 Trim the asparagus and use a potato peeler to peel about 5 cm (2 inches) off the base of each stalk. Arrange the asparagus in a single layer in a shallow roasting tin.
2 Spoon 4 tablespoons of the olive oil over the asparagus and shake lightly to mix. Roast in a preheated oven, 200°C (400°F), Gas Mark 6, for about 20 minutes, until just tender, turning the asparagus once during cooking. Leave to cool.
3 Transfer the roasted asparagus spears to a shallow dish, spoon the remaining olive oil and the lime juice over the top. Sprinkle with the salt and pepper and toss lightly. Garnish with torn coriander leaves.

Serves 4-6
Preparation time: 10 minutes
Cooking time: about 20 minutes
Oven temperature: 200°C (400°F),
Gas Mark 6

Greek Salad

750 g/1½ lb tomatoes, sliced
1 small onion, thinly sliced
1 small cucumber, peeled
1 green pepper, cored, deseeded and
   thinly sliced
125 g/4 oz black olives
250 g/8 oz feta cheese
flat leaf parsley leaves, roughly torn
salt and pepper
DRESSING:
9 tablespoons extra-virgin olive oil
3 tablespoons lemon juice
pinch of sugar
1 tablespoon chopped fresh oregano

1 Arrange the tomatoes, overlapping slightly, in slices in concentric circles in a large serving bowl or on individual plates. Scatter the onion slices on top of the tomatoes.
2 Halve the cucumber lengthways and cut into slices. Add to the salad with the green pepper and black olives. Crumble the feta cheese and scatter over the salad with the parsley. Season sparingly with salt (the amount required will depend on how salty the feta is) and grind a little black pepper over the top.
3 To make the dressing, whisk all the ingredients together in a small bowl or place in a screw-top jar, close the lid tightly and shake to combine. Pour over the salad and serve.

Serves 4-6
Preparation time: 20 minutes

Mediterranean Vegetable Salad

Grilling the vegetables brings out their flavour to create a salad which evokes memories of freshly picked, sun-warmed Mediterranean courgettes, peppers and tomatoes.

2 small fennel bulbs
2 red onions
3 courgettes
4 tablespoons extra-virgin olive oil
1 teaspoon finely grated lemon rind
1 tablespoon chopped fresh thyme
1 red or yellow pepper, cored, deseeded and cut into wide strips
175 g/6 oz cherry tomatoes, halved
DRESSING:
4 tablespoons extra-virgin olive oil
2 tablespoons lemon juice
pinch of sugar
1 tablespoon chopped fresh oregano
salt and pepper

1 Cut the fennel bulbs and red onions into wedges, leaving the root ends intact to prevent them from falling apart during cooking. Halve the courgettes, then slice them thinly lengthways.

2 Bring a large saucepan of water to the boil. Add the fennel and onions. When the water returns to the boil, cook the vegetables for 1 minute. Add the courgette strips and cook for 1 minute more. Drain in a colander and refresh under cold running water, then drain thoroughly and set aside.

3 Combine the olive oil, lemon rind and thyme in a large bowl. Add all the vegetables and toss lightly to coat them in the flavoured oil.

4 Line a grill pan with foil. Spread the vegetable mixture evenly in a single layer in the grill pan. Cook under a preheated hot grill for 15-20 minutes, turning frequently, until the vegetables are tender and patched with brown. Allow the mixture to cool.

5 Arrange the cooled vegetables on a serving platter. Make the dressing by whisking all the ingredients together in a small bowl. Alternatively place them in a screw-top jar, close the lid tightly and shake to combine. Pour the dressing over the vegetables and serve.

Serves 4
Preparation time: 25 minutes
Cooking time: about 20 minutes

Beefsteak Tomato Salad

The dressing for this salad is simply good-quality olive oil flavoured with herbs and the juices from the tomatoes. I sometimes splash over a few drops of balsamic vinegar too, if I have it, but either way this salad is good enough to need lots of crusty bread as an accompaniment to mop up the dressing.

4 beefsteak tomatoes, sliced
5 tablespoons extra-virgin olive oil
2 spring onions, finely chopped
2 tablespoons chopped fresh oregano
    or marjoram

few sprigs of basil, roughly torn
50 g/2 oz black olives
coarse sea salt and pepper

1 Arrange the tomatoes, overlapping slightly, in concentric circles on a large platter. Drizzle the olive oil carefully over the top of the tomatoes and add salt and pepper to taste.
2 Sprinkle the spring onions over the tomatoes, together with the oregano or marjoram and the basil. Scatter the olives over the top. Leave the salad to stand for at least 15 minutes before serving.

Serves 4
Preparation time: 15 minutes, plus standing time

Two Tomato and Mozzarella Salad

500 g/1 lb plum tomatoes, sliced
1 tablespoon chopped fresh oregano
375 g/12 oz mozzarella cheese,
    preferably made from buffalo milk
12 sun-dried tomatoes preserved in oil,
    drained and sliced in strips
few sprigs of basil, roughly torn
salt and pepper
DRESSING:
5 tablespoons extra-virgin olive oil
3 tablespoons oil from the sun-dried
    tomatoes
3 tablespoons red wine vinegar
½ garlic clove, crushed
pinch of sugar

1 Arrange the plum tomato slices in a single layer on a large platter. Sprinkle with salt and pepper to taste, together with the oregano.
2 To make the dressing, whisk all the ingredients together in a small bowl, or place in a screw-top jar, close the lid tightly and shake to combine.
3 Slice the mozzarella and arrange on top of the sliced plum tomatoes. Tuck the sun-dried tomato strips between them. Scatter the torn basil over the top.
4 Whisk or shake the dressing again, then pour over the salad and serve.

Serves 4
Preparation time: 15 minutes

Grilled Aubergine Salad

2 aubergines, trimmed
2 teaspoons salt
1 quantity Classic French Dressing (see page 54)
3 spring onions, finely chopped
sprigs of fresh herbs (e.g. thyme, dill, parsley, coriander, basil, chives)
pepper

1 Cut the aubergines into slices about 1 cm (½ inch) thick. Arrange in a colander and sprinkle with the salt. Set the colander over a bowl or in the sink and leave for 30-40 minutes to allow the bitter juices from the aubergines to run out.

2 Rinse the aubergine slices under cold running water, drain and pat dry with kitchen paper. Arrange in a single layer on a baking sheet. Brush with a little of the dressing. Cook under a preheated hot grill for about 5 minutes, turning once, until browned on both sides, then transfer to a shallow serving bowl.

3 Add the spring onions to the bowl and season with pepper. Spoon over the remaining dressing and toss lightly. Leave until cold, then sprinkle over the herbs before serving.

Serves 6
Preparation time: 15 minutes, plus standing time
Cooking time: 5 minutes

Raw Onion Salad

You could serve this salad as an accompaniment to dishes with an Indian flavour such as chicken or lamb tikka or with poppadums and mango chutney. The flavour of the onion compliments the spices.

2 red onions or mild yellow onions
2 tomatoes, skinned, seeded and
  chopped
1 teaspoon ground cumin
½ teaspoon mild chilli powder
2 tablespoons lemon juice
2-3 tablespoons chopped fresh
  coriander
salt

1 Cut the onions in half, then slice very thinly. Put the slices in a bowl. Add the remaining ingredients and toss well. Leave to stand for at least 15 minutes before serving.

Serves 4-6
Preparation time: 15 minutes, plus standing time

Cucumber and Dill Salad

A delicate, summery salad, this makes a perfect accompaniment to grilled or barbecued fish and chicken.

1 cucumber, peeled and very thinly sliced
2 teaspoons salt
sprigs of dill, to garnish

DRESSING:
4 tablespoons thick natural yogurt or Greek yogurt
1 teaspoon white wine vinegar
2 tablespoons chopped fresh dill
pepper

1 Put the cucumber slices in a colander set over a large plate or in the sink. Sprinkle the salt over the cucumber and leave to stand for 20-30 minutes, to allow the excess moisture to drain away. Rinse the cucumber under cold running water, then drain thoroughly and place in a shallow serving dish.
2 To make the dressing, stir all the ingredients together in a small bowl.
3 Spoon the dressing over the cucumber and toss lightly to mix. Garnish with sprigs of dill and serve.

Serves 4-6
Preparation time: 15 minutes, plus standing time

VARIATIONS

Minted Cucumber Salad

Replace the dill in the dressing with chopped fresh mint. Garnish with sprigs of mint.

Prawn or Salmon and Cucumber Salad

With the addition of fish or shellfish, this becomes an elegant first course.

Prepare the salad as in the main recipe and top with 375-625 g/ 12 oz-1¼ lb cooked peeled prawns or poached salmon. Squeeze a little lemon juice over the fish and garnish with dill sprigs.

Cucumber and Strawberry Salad

This refreshing salad epitomizes a perfect summer's day. Serve it with cold salmon or on its own as a light starter.

1 small cucumber, peeled and very thinly sliced

1 tablespoon grapeseed oil or light olive oil
1 teaspoon white wine vinegar
250 g/8 oz strawberries, hulled and thinly sliced
salt and pepper
mint leaves and edible flowers, to garnish

1 Place the cucumber slices in a bowl. Add the oil and vinegar, with salt and pepper to taste. Toss lightly.

2 Arrange the cucumber and strawberry slices on a serving platter or individual plates. Scatter a few mint leaves and edible flowers on top. Chill for at least 30 minutes before serving.

Serves 4
Preparation time: 15 minutes, plus chilling time

Globe Artichokes with Garlic and Herb Mayonnaise

4 globe artichokes
1 lemon, quartered
4 tablespoons olive oil
1 quantity Garlic and Herb Mayonnaise
(see page 95)
salt and pepper
lemon wedges, to garnish

1 Discard the large base stalks from the artichokes and rub the cut surface with lemon to prevent discolouring.
2 Bring a large saucepan of water to the boil. Add the artichokes. Squeeze the juice from the lemon quarters into the pan and drop the pieces in too. Cook the artichokes for 25-30 minutes, until a leaf can be pulled out easily. Using a slotted spoon, transfer the artichokes to a board and leave upside down to drain and cool slightly.
3 Cut each artichoke into 4 wedges. Discard the hairy choke.
4 Arrange the artichoke quarters on individual plates or a large platter. Drizzle the olive oil over, and add salt and pepper. Serve with garlic and herb mayonnaise for dipping. Garnish with lemon wedges.

Serves 4
Preparation time: 15 minutes
Cooking time: 25-30 minutes

French Bean and Apricot Salad

A pretty salad to make the most of the all-too-brief season for fresh apricots, with toasted almonds to bring out the apricots' flavour.

500 g/1 lb French beans, topped
  and tailed
6 ripe apricots, halved, stoned
  and sliced
few sprigs of parsley, roughly torn
1 tablespoon chopped fresh tarragon

1 quantity Classic French Dressing (see
  page 54) or 1 quantity Tarragon
  and Orange Dressing (see page 18)
salt and pepper
about 25 g/1 oz almond flakes,
  toasted, to garnish

1 Bring a saucepan of water to the boil, add the beans and cook for 2-3 minutes, or until just tender. Drain in a colander, refresh under cold running water and drain again. Blot the excess water with kitchen paper and place the beans in a serving bowl.
2 Add the sliced apricots to the bowl with the beans, then add the herbs. Season with salt and pepper.
3 Add the dressing to the salad and toss lightly. Garnish with a sprinkling of toasted almond flakes.

Serves 4-6
Preparation time: 10 minutes
Cooking time: 3 minutes

French Bean Salad with Ham

It is the quality of the ham that determines whether this salad is merely good or sensational. Home-boiled or roasted ham will make a superb dish, otherwise use premium-quality ham cut in thick slices.

375 g/12 oz French beans, topped
  and tailed
250 g/8 oz cooked ham
4 spring onions, finely chopped
2 tablespoons chopped fresh parsley
1 quantity Classic French Dressing (see
  page 54)
salt and pepper
few salad leaves, to garnish (optional)

1 Cook and drain the beans as in the main recipe.
2 Using two forks, shred the ham. Add to the beans with the spring onions, parsley, salt and pepper.
3 Pour the dressing over the salad and toss lightly. Serve from the bowl or arrange on individual plates. Garnish with a few salad leaves.

Serves 4
Preparation time: 15 minutes
Cooking time: 2-3 minutes

Emerald Green Salad

1 cos lettuce
2 ripe avocados
2 tablespoons lemon juice
3 kiwifruit
2 tablespoons chopped fresh mixed
  herbs (mint, parsley, basil, chives)

2 spring onions, sliced
1 quantity Classic French Dressing (see
  page 54)

1 Tear the lettuce into bite-sized pieces and place in a large bowl.
2 Halve, stone and peel the avocados. Chop the flesh and place in a bowl with the lemon juice. Toss well, then add to the salad bowl.

3 Peel the kiwifruit and cut length-ways into thin wedges. Add to the salad with the chopped herbs and spring onions.
4 Pour the dressing over the salad and toss lightly.

Serves 4-6
Preparation time: 15 minutes

Jersey Royal and Celery Salad

500 g/1 lb small Jersey Royal potatoes, scrubbed
6 celery sticks, with leaves if possible
75 g/3 oz black olives
3 tablespoons capers, rinsed and drained
few sprigs of parsley, roughly chopped
1 quantity Tarragon and Lemon Dressing (see page 18)
salt and pepper

1 Bring a saucepan of water to the boil. Add the potatoes and cook for about 12 minutes, until just tender. Drain in a colander and refresh under cold running water. Drain thoroughly and leave to cool.
2 Slice the celery sticks diagonally and roughly chop any leaves. Place in a bowl with the olives, capers and parsley. Add the cooled potatoes and season with salt and pepper.
3 Pour the dressing over the salad, toss well and serve.

Serves 4-6
Preparation time: 20 minutes
Cooking time: about 12 minutes

Mangetout, Mushroom and Corn Salad

This combination of crisp textures and makes a fine accompaniment to chicken and seafood. The salad is also good made with Garlic and Herb Mayonnaise or – for the calorie-conscious – with Yogurt Dressing and fresh herbs.

250 g/8 oz mangetout, topped and
   tailed
175 g/6 oz baby corn cobs
175 g/6 oz button mushrooms, thinly
   sliced

1 small red onion
1 quantity Sweet Pepper Dressing (see
   page 103)
salt and pepper
roughly torn parsley leaves, to garnish

1 Cut the mangetout in half diagonally. Bring a saucepan of water to the boil, add the mangetout and cook for 30 seconds only. Drain in a colander, refresh under cold running water, then drain again thoroughly.
2 Cook the corn cobs in a saucepan of boiling water for 3 minutes, until barely tender. Drain, refresh under cold running water, then drain thoroughly.
3 Place the button mushrooms in a salad bowl with the mangetout and corn. Cut the red onion into thin wedges and separate the layers. Add to the salad with salt and pepper to taste. Toss lightly.
4 Serve the salad on individual plates, and spoon the dressing on to the side of the plates. Garnish with torn parsley leaves.

Serves 4-6
Preparation time: 15 minutes
Cooking time: 3-4 minutes

Melon and Parma Ham

1 small Charantais melon
1 small Galia or Ogen melon
12 thin slices of Parma ham
sprigs of mint, to garnish
DRESSING:
75 g/3 oz dolcelatte cheese
2 tablespoons lemon juice
5 tablespoons milk
2 tablespoons chopped fresh mint
salt and pepper

1 Start by making the dressing. Put the cheese in a small bowl. Add the lemon juice and mash to a paste, using a fork. Stir in the milk and mint, with salt and pepper to taste.
2 Cut the melons in half and discard the seeds. Peel the flesh and slice into thin wedges. Alternatively slice 1 melon and use a melon baller to scoop the flesh of the other. Arrange the melon on individual serving plates with the Parma ham.
3 Just before serving, spoon the dressing over and around the melon. Garnish with sprigs of mint.

Serves 4-6
Preparation time: 15 minutes

Cucumber and Pineapple Salad with Guacamole

This cooling salad is the perfect accompaniment to hot Mexican-style dishes. Make the guacamole just before serving as it tends to discolour if left to stand. If you have to make the guacamole in advance, put the avocado stone back into the middle of the guacamole and cover with clingfilm, to lessen the discoloration.

½ cucumber, peeled and very thinly sliced
1 teaspoon salt
½ ripe pineapple, peeled, cored and cut into bite-sized pieces
bunch of fresh coriander
salt and pepper
GUACAMOLE:
2 ripe avocados, roughly chopped
1 garlic clove, crushed
juice of 1 lime
1 red chilli, finely chopped
1 tomato, finely chopped
2 spring onions, finely chopped

1 Put the cucumber slices in a colander and sprinkle with the salt. Leave to drain over a large plate or in the sink for 20 minutes.
2 Place the pineapple in a bowl. Roughly tear about half of the coriander leaves into the bowl.

3 Rinse the cucumber under cold running water. Drain well, blot dry with kitchen paper, then add to the pineapple. Season and toss lightly.
4 To make the guacamole, place all the ingredients in a bowl. Using a fork, mash together thoroughly. Season to taste. Serve at once, with the salad, garnished with coriander.

Serves 4-6
Preparation time: 20 minutes

Leeks Vinaigrette

You can serve this as a starter with some good brown bread, or as a side salad. If you cannot get very young leeks – not much fatter than a pencil – use 4 medium-sized leeks and slice them in half lengthways.

24 very young leeks
1 hard-boiled egg, finely chopped
1 tablespoon chopped fresh parsley
2 tablespoons chopped walnuts
salt and pepper
VINAIGRETTE:
4 tablespoons extra-virgin olive oil
1 tablespoon white wine vinegar
½ teaspoon Dijon mustard

1 Rinse the leeks thoroughly to remove any dirt. Boil them in shallow water in a frying pan or steam until just tender. Drain thoroughly.
2 Meanwhile, make the vinaigrette. Whisk together all the ingredients in a small bowl or shake together in a screw-top jar until combined. Season with salt and pepper.
3 Transfer the drained leeks, while still hot, to a shallow serving dish. Pour over the vinaigrette and leave to cool. Just before serving, sprinkle with the chopped egg, parsley and walnuts.

Serves 4
Preparation time: 10 minutes
Cooking time: 3-5 minutes

Baked Beetroot with Soured Cream and Onion Rings

4 raw beetroot (unpeeled)
3 tablespoons light olive oil
1 large onion, sliced
about 50 g/2 oz rocket
few dill sprigs
1 dessert apple
2 teaspoons lemon juice
150 ml/¼ pint soured cream
salt and pepper
beetroot leaves, to garnish (optional)

1 Wrap each beetroot individually in foil and place on a baking sheet. Bake in a preheated oven, 200°C (400°F), Gas Mark 6, for 40-50 minutes, or until tender.
2 Meanwhile, heat the oil in a frying pan. Add the onion slices and cook over a fairly high heat for about 5 minutes, stirring frequently, until browned and beginning to crisp. Transfer to kitchen paper to drain.
3 Just before serving, arrange the rocket and dill on 4 serving plates. Peel and core the apple and finely dice the flesh. Place in a bowl with the lemon juice and toss well to

prevent discolouring. Divide the diced apple between the plates.
4 To serve, remove the cooked beetroot from their foil wrappings. Put one on each plate and cut in half or quarters. Serve with soured cream, and scatter the fried onion around the beetroot. Season to taste with salt and pepper. Garnish with beetroot leaves, if liked.

Serves 4
Preparation time: 15 minutes
Cooking time: 40-50 minutes
Oven temperature: 200°C (400°F), Gas Mark 6

Winter Vegetable Platter with Rouille

selection of winter vegetables (e.g. potatoes, parsnips, kohlrabi, baby turnips, leeks, Jerusalem artichokes, celeriac, carrots)

extra-virgin olive oil
coarse sea salt
fresh herb sprigs, to garnish
ROUILLE:
1 red pepper, deseeded and chopped
2 garlic cloves, chopped
2 red chillies, deseeded and chopped
6 tablespoons extra-virgin olive oil
25 g/1 oz fresh white breadcrumbs
salt and pepper

1 First prepare the rouille: put the pepper, garlic, chillies and olive oil in a liquidizer or food processor and process until fairly smooth. Clean down the sides of the bowl with a spatula occasionally to make sure you blend all the ingredients evenly. Add the breadcrumbs, and salt and pepper to taste, and process again to form a thick paste. Transfer to a small bowl, cover and chill until ready to serve.

2 Prepare the vegetables according to type and size – the dish will look more attractive if all the vegetables are of a similar size, or are cut into similarly sized pieces. Boil or steam the vegetables until just tender. Drain and refresh under cold running water, then drain thoroughly.

3 Arrange the vegetables on a large serving platter. Drizzle with olive oil and sprinkle with sea salt. Serve with the rouille, garnished with sprigs of fresh herbs.

Serves 4-6
Preparation time: 30 minutes
Cooking time: 20-30 minutes

New Potato Salad with Wholegrain Mustard Cream

This salad is a favourite served with grilled foods such as steaks, salmon, trout, vegetables and goats' cheese. Vegetarians can omit the Parma ham or replace it with shredded spring onions, capers or chopped walnut pieces.

750 g/1½ lb small new potatoes	salt and pepper
50 g/2 oz thinly sliced Parma ham	TO GARNISH:
150 ml/¼ pint double cream	flat leaf parsley, roughly torn (optional)
2 tablespoons wholegrain mustard	chive flowers (optional)

1 Cook the potatoes, whole, in a pan of boiling water for about 15 minutes, until tender. Drain and rinse briefly in cold water. Drain thoroughly and transfer to a bowl to cool slightly.

2 Grill the Parma ham under a preheated hot grill for 2-2 ½ minutes, turning once, until crisp and golden. Set aside.

3 In a small bowl, stir together the cream and mustard until the mixture begins to thicken. Mix with the potatoes while they are still warm, adding salt and pepper to taste.

4 Serve the salad warm or cold with the reserved Parma ham crumbled over. Sprinkle with roughly torn parsley leaves or scatter with chive flowers, if liked.

Serves 4-6
Preparation time: 8 minutes
Cooking time: 15 minutes

VARIATION

Replace the mustard cream dressing with Horseradish and Soured Cream Dressing (see right).

Horseradish and Soured Cream Dressing

This is the simplest of dressings but it really is delicious and very versatile. Use it as it is with winter vegetables, roast meat and smoked fish. Alternatively, add chopped fresh herbs, chopped toasted nuts, finely chopped garlic or onion, pimientos, capers or olives.

300 ml/½ pint soured cream
4 teaspoons creamed horseradish
salt and pepper

1 Stir the soured cream and creamed horseradish together in a bowl or jug. Add salt and pepper to taste.

Makes 300 ml/½ pint
Preparation time: 1 minute

Classic Potato Salad

Choose potato varieties with a waxy texture, such as Charlotte or Pink Fir Apple. They will retain their shape better than floury baking potatoes.

750 g/1½ lb waxy salad potatoes
4 spring onions, finely chopped
2 tablespoons snipped fresh chives
salt and pepper
DRESSING:
6 tablespoons Mayonnaise (see page 15)
3 tablespoons single cream
1 teaspoon Dijon mustard

1 Cook the potatoes, whole and in their skins, in a large pan of boiling water for about 15 minutes, or until tender. Drain and refresh under cold running water then drain thoroughly and allow to cool.
2 Thickly slice the potatoes and place in a serving bowl with the chopped spring onions. Add salt and pepper to taste.
3 To make the dressing, stir together the mayonnaise, cream and mustard. Spoon over the salad and toss lightly to mix. Serve the salad sprinkled with the snipped chives.

Serves 6
Preparation time: 15 minutes
Cooking time: about 15 minutes

VARIATION

Potato Salad with Dill Pickle and Anchovy or Pimiento

Finely slice 1 dill pickle and add to the salad with the potatoes and spring onions. Just before serving, decorate the top of the salad with anchovy fillets or strips of pimiento and sprinkle with chives as above.

Beetroot Vinaigrette

A colourful side salad of beetroot, dried apricots and spring onions with a simple vinaigrette dressing.

500 g/1 lb cooked beetroot
75 g/3 oz ready-to-eat dried apricots
2 spring onions, shredded
DRESSING:
4 tablespoons olive or grapeseed oil
4 teaspoons red wine vinegar
1 teaspoon Dijon mustard
pinch of sugar
salt and pepper

1 Cut the beetroot into 1 cm (½ inch) dice and place in a shallow bowl. Finely dice the apricots and add to the bowl.

2 To make the dressing, whisk all the ingredients together in a small bowl or shake together in a screw-top jar until combined.

3 To serve, pour the dressing over the beetroot mixture and toss lightly to mix. Top with the shredded spring onions.

Serves 4-6
Preparation time: 15 minutes

Sweet Potato and Grilled Chilli Salad

750 g/1½ lb sweet potatoes, peeled
   and sliced
3 large red chillies
6 tablespoons groundnut oil, for frying
a handful of coriander leaves, torn
coarse sea salt and pepper
50 g/2 oz lamb's lettuce or rocket

DRESSING:

1 teaspoon finely grated lime rind
2 tablespoons lime juice
4 tablespoons groundnut oil
2 tablespoons sesame oil
   or 8 tablespoons Ginger and Lime
   Dressing (see right)

1 Preheat the grill to hot.
2 Parboil the sweet potato slices in a large pan of boiling water for about
5 minutes. Drain the potatoes well and then refresh under cold running water.
Spread out on kitchen paper to dry.
3 Meanwhile, cook the chillies under the preheated hot grill, turning
frequently, until the skin is blistered and blackened all over. Allow to cool
slightly, then carefully remove and discard the skin and seeds. Cut the flesh
into thin strips and set aside.
4 Heat 3 tablespoons of the groundnut oil in a large frying pan. Sauté the
sweet potato slices in batches over a medium-high heat until crisp and lightly
browned. Transfer to a large shallow serving bowl as they are done and add
more oil to the pan as necessary.
5 To make the dressing, mix all the ingredients together in a small bowl until
thoroughly blended or shake together in a screw-top jar.
6 Add the chilli strips and coriander to the salad bowl. Season with coarse
sea salt and pepper to taste. Toss lightly to mix.
7 Just before serving, pour over the dressing and toss well. Serve with the
lamb's lettuce or rocket.

Serves 4
Preparation time: 15 minutes
Cooking time: about 20 minutes

Ginger and Lime Dressing

*This dressing has a fresh
oriental flavour that is good
with fish and shellfish, duck and
chicken as well as many leafy
salads and lightly cooked
vegetables. You can prepare it
ahead but should add the
coriander just before serving.*

2 teaspoons grated fresh root ginger
1 garlic clove, crushed
2 limes
1 tablespoon clear honey
75 ml/3 fl oz groundnut or
   grapeseed oil
2 tablespoons chopped fresh coriander
salt and pepper

1 Combine the ginger and garlic
together in a bowl. Grate the limes
finely and add the rind to the bowl
with the honey. Stir in salt and
pepper to taste.
2 Squeeze the juice from both limes.
Add to the bowl and beat well with
a balloon whisk or wooden spoon.
Pour in the oil, whisking the dressing
until well mixed. Just before using, stir
in the chopped coriander.

Makes about 150 ml/¼ pint
Preparation time: 10 minutes

Leek and Mushroom Salad with Bacon and Croûtons

175 g/6 oz button mushrooms
375 g/12 oz trimmed leeks
2 thick slices white bread, crusts removed
4 tablespoons olive oil
3 rashers of streaky bacon, diced
1-2 garlic cloves
1 teaspoon salt
flat leaf parsley, roughly torn

BALSAMIC VINEGAR DRESSING:
3 tablespoons olive oil
2 tablespoons balsamic vinegar
2 tablespoons Dijon or wholegrain mustard
pepper
or about 6 tablespoons Classic French Dressing (see page 54)
or Walnut Dressing (see page 42)

1 If the mushrooms are tiny, leave them whole; cut the larger mushrooms into quarters. Cut the leeks into 7 cm (3 inch) lengths, then cut lengthways into julienne strips. Cut the bread into small cubes or other shapes.

2 Blanch the leeks very briefly in a saucepan of boiling water, until just wilted. Refresh under cold running water and drain thoroughly. Transfer to a shallow bowl.

3 Heat 2 tablespoons of the olive oil in a frying pan. Add the diced bacon and cook for 2 minutes, until just beginning to crisp, then remove from the pan with a slotted spoon and set aside in a small bowl.

4 Add the mushrooms to the pan and cook over a high heat for about 2 minutes, stirring, until browned. Add the mushrooms to bowl with the bacon.

5 To make the dressing, put all the ingredients into a small bowl and whisk until thoroughly blended. Alternatively, shake the ingredients together in a screw-top jar.

6 Just before serving, crush the garlic with the salt. Add the remaining oil to the frying pan. Fry the bread shapes, stirring for a few seconds, until beginning to brown. Add the garlic and continue cooking and stirring until the croûtons are golden.

7 To serve, add two-thirds of the dressing to the leeks and toss well. Add the remaining dressing to the bacon and mushrooms and toss gently. Divide the leeks and the bacon mixture between 4 plates, and sprinkle the hot croûtons and the parsley over the top.

Serves 4
Preparation time: 20 minutes
Cooking time: about 8 minutes

Wild Mushroom Salad with Croûtons

If you are lucky enough to be able to pick your own wild mushrooms, use them to make this salad; otherwise you can find wild mushrooms for sale in some specialist shops. Alternatively, use a mixture of cultivated mushrooms, such as oyster, chestnut, shiitake, which are sold in many supermarkets.

500 g/1 lb mixed wild mushrooms (e.g. chanterelles, ceps, morels, field or horse mushrooms)
or cultivated types (e.g. oyster, shiitake, chestnut or flat mushrooms)
4 tablespoons olive oil
1 shallot, finely chopped
1 garlic clove, chopped
1 teaspoon chopped fresh thyme
4 tablespoons water
about 50 g/2 oz rocket or watercress
handful of basil leaves, roughly torn
250 g/8 oz Croûtons (see page 23)
salt and pepper
6 tablespoons Classic French Dressing (see page 54)
or Horseradish and Soured Cream Dressing (see page 87)
chopped parsley, to garnish (optional)

1 Prepare the mushrooms: leave small mushrooms whole but slice or chop the larger varieties.

2 Heat the olive oil in a large frying pan. Add the shallot and cook over a medium heat for 3-4 minutes, until softened. Stir in the garlic and cook for a further 1 minute.

3 Add the mushrooms and thyme to the pan. Season with salt and pepper and cook, stirring, for 2 minutes. Add the water and cook over a fairly high heat for about 5 minutes, stirring frequently, until the mushrooms are tender. Transfer to a bowl and leave to cool.

4 When the mushroom mixture has cooled add the rocket or watercress, torn basil leaves and croûtons to the bowl. Toss lightly to mix. Drizzle the chosen dressing over the salad and serve at once, sprinkled with chopped parsley, if liked.

Serves 4
Preparation time: 15 minutes
Cooking time: about 12 minutes

Winter Vegetable Julienne with Aïoli and Spiced Nuts

The three elements of this salad complement one another perfectly: crisp julienne vegetables, crunchy spiced nuts and melt-in-the-mouth aïoli. You can use any combination of winter vegetables – try kohlrabi or winter radish (mooli).

300 g/10 oz carrots
300 g/10 oz leeks
250 g/8 oz celeriac
2 teaspoons lemon juice
1 quantity Aïoli (Garlic Mayonnaise)
   (see right)

SPICED NUTS:
1 tablespoon groundnut oil
2 teaspoons mustard seeds
1 tablespoon chopped hazelnuts
1 tablespoon chopped almonds
2 tablespoons chopped fresh parsley
coarse sea salt and pepper

1 First prepare the spiced nuts. Heat the oil in a small saucepan and add the mustard seeds. Cook over a high heat for a few seconds, until the seeds begin to pop, then stir in the nuts and cook, stirring, until lightly browned. Stir in the chopped parsley and remove from the heat. Season with coarse sea salt and pepper.

2 Peel and trim all the vegetables and cut into julienne strips; as you cut the celeriac, drop the strips into a bowl with the lemon juice and toss well – this will prevent discoloration, as well as adding flavour.

3 Divide the vegetables between 4 serving plates. Spoon a little aïoli on to each plate, and sprinkle with the spiced nuts.

Serves 4
Preparation time: 25 minutes
Cooking time: about 3 minutes

Aïoli

Aïoli is a Provençal variation on mayonnaise, strongly flavoured with garlic.

Make a basic mayonnaise (see page 15). Put the mayonnaise in a bowl and stir in 2 crushed garlic cloves. Leave the aïoli to stand for at least 30 minutes before serving, to allow the full flavour of the garlic to permeate the mayonnaise.

VARIATION

Garlic and Herb Mayonnaise

Make as for the Aïoli, adding 2 tablespoons of finely chopped mixed fresh herbs (e.g. chives, tarragon, parsley, dill, oregano) to the mayonnaise with the garlic. Leave to stand for at least 30 minutes before serving.

Mushroom and Butter Bean Salad

250 g/8 oz dried butter beans, soaked
    overnight
250 g/8 oz button mushrooms
1-2 tablespoons snipped fresh chives
large handful of flat leaf parsley,
    roughly torn
50 g/2 oz Parmesan cheese (optional)
DRESSING:
5 tablespoons extra-virgin olive oil
½ garlic clove, crushed
1 teaspoon finely grated lemon rind
2 tablespoons lemon juice
½ teaspoon mustard
pinch of sugar
salt and pepper

1 Put the soaked butter beans in a large saucepan with plenty of cold water. Bring to the boil and boil briskly for 10 minutes, then lower the heat, cover and simmer for 30-40 minutes, until the beans are tender. Drain and rinse under cold running water, then drain thoroughly and leave to cool.

2 To make the dressing, whisk all the ingredients together in a small bowl until thoroughly blended, or shake the ingredients together in a screw-top jar until combined.

3.Thinly slice the button mushrooms and place in a large bowl. Add the cooled butter beans and pour over the dressing. Toss well to mix and leave to stand for at least 20 minutes before serving.

4 To serve, sprinkle the chives and parsley over the salad and toss lightly. If liked, use a potato peeler or a small sharp knife to pare wafer-thin slices of Parmesan over the top.

Serves 4-6
Preparation time: 15 minutes, plus overnight soaking and standing time
Cooking time: 40-50 minutes

Red Cabbage, Apple and Wensleydale Salad

50 g/2 oz pecan nuts or walnuts, roughly chopped
1 small red cabbage
1 red or white onion, thinly sliced
175 g/6 oz fresh dates, pitted and roughly chopped
1 large red apple, cored, halved and thinly sliced
150 g/5 oz Wensleydale cheese
salt and pepper
1 quantity Sweet Mustard Dressing (see below)

1 Place the pecans or walnuts on a baking sheet and toast under a pre-heated hot grill for 2-3 minutes, until browned. Set aside.
2 Shred the cabbage as finely as possible and place in a large salad bowl with the onion, dates and apple. Season with salt and pepper and toss lightly to mix.
3 Crumble the Wensleydale over the salad and sprinkle over the reserved toasted nuts. Drizzle the dressing over and serve at once.

Serves 4-6
Preparation time: 15 minutes
Cooking time: 2-3 minutes

Sweet Mustard Dressing

3 tablespoons olive oil
2 tablespoons wholegrain mustard
1 tablespoon clear honey
1 teaspoon white wine vinegar or lemon juice
salt and pepper

1 Place all the ingredients in a small bowl and whisk with a balloon whisk until thoroughly blended.
Alternatively, put all the ingredients together in a screw-top jar, close the lid tightly and shake until thoroughly combined.

Makes 75 ml/3 fl oz
Preparation time: 2 minutes

Deborah's Warm Potato and Pancetta Salad

This aromatic potato salad is delicious on it own, as a side dish, or perhaps with one or two other root vegetable salads.

500 g/1 lb small new potatoes
2 red onions
4 sprigs of rosemary
6 tablespoons extra-virgin
   olive oil

75 g/3 oz smoked pancetta, in thick
   slices, cut into strips
3 tablespoons red wine vinegar
coarse sea salt and pepper

1 Add the potatoes to a pan of boiling water and parboil for 5 minutes. Drain thoroughly and transfer to a roasting tin.
2 Cut the red onions into wedges, leaving the root ends intact so that the layers do not separate. Add to the roasting tin with the rosemary. Drizzle over 4 tablespoons of the olive oil. Place the roasting tin in a preheated oven, 200°C (400°F), Gas Mark 6, and roast for 45-60 minutes, until the potatoes are tender and lightly patched with brown.
3 When the potatoes are done, heat the remaining 2 tablespoons of olive oil in a frying pan. Add the pancetta and fry until crisp and lightly browned. Add the red wine vinegar and bring to the boil, stirring, to deglaze the pan. Pour over the potatoes and toss to coat. Season with coarse sea salt and pepper. Serve warm or cold, discarding the rosemary stalks just before serving.

Serves 4
Preparation time: 15 minutes
Cooking time: 45-60 minutes
Oven temperature: 200°C (400°F), Gas Mark 6

Swede and Watercress Salad

625 g/1¼ lb swede
1 large red pepper
6 rashers of smoked streaky bacon
50 g/2 oz watercress
1 tablespoon snipped fresh chives
1 quantity French Dressing (see page 54)

1 Cut the swede into 1 cm (½ inch) dice. Cook in boiling water for about 5 minutes, until just tender. Drain and refresh under cold running water, then drain thoroughly and transfer to a serving bowl.

2 Meanwhile, grill the pepper under a preheated hot grill for about 15 minutes, turning frequently, until the skin is blistered and blackened all over. Remove to a plate and allow to cool slightly. Place the bacon rashers under the grill and cook until crisp.

3 Remove the charred skin from the pepper and discard. Cut the pepper in half and remove the core and seeds. Reserve any juice from the inside of the pepper, adding it to the bowl with the swede. Cut the pepper into thin strips and add to the swede. Dice the bacon and add to the salad, together with the watercress. Toss lightly to mix.

4 Pour the dressing over the salad and toss lightly. Serve sprinkled with snipped fresh chives.

Serves 4-6
Preparation time: 15 minutes
Cooking time: 15-20 minutes

Warm Baby Turnips with Mustard Dressing

Use the smallest baby turnips you can find for this salad – buy them with their tops still on if possible. Serve as an accompaniment to rich meats such as duck, goose, lamb or beef, or with chicken.

500 g/1 lb baby turnips
1 red onion, thinly sliced
handful of flat leaf parsley, roughly torn
coarse sea salt and pepper
1 quantity Sweet Mustard Dressing (see page 97)

1 Cook the baby turnips in a pan of boiling water for 8-10 minutes; they should still be slightly crisp. Drain and refresh under cold running water, then drain thoroughly.

2 Put the turnips and onion slices in a serving bowl. Season with coarse sea salt and pepper. Pour the dressing over the turnips and toss well. Serve warm, sprinkled with roughly torn parsley.

Serves 4-6
Preparation time: 10 minutes
Cooking time: 8-10 minutes

Celeriac and Stilton Salad

Serve this salad as a main course with some good crusty bread to make the most of the cheese and the Sweet Pepper Dressing. You could also serve it as an accompaniment to chicken, fish or shellfish.

300 g/10 oz celeriac
4 teaspoons lemon juice
1 bunch watercress
1 head chicory, separated into leaves
1 small cos lettuce, roughly torn
1 small red onion, thinly sliced
250 g/8 oz Stilton, cut into small cubes

75 g/3 oz salted cashew nuts
handful of flat leaf parsley, roughly
  torn
salt and pepper
1 quantity Sweet Pepper Dressing
  (see right)

1 Peel and coarsely shred the celeriac – shredding celeriac is easy if you have a food processor. Place the shredded celeriac in a bowl and add the lemon juice. Toss together well to prevent discolouring.
2 Arrange the salad leaves on individual serving plates together with the celeriac and onion slices. Scatter the Stilton over each salad, then sprinkle the cashew nuts and torn parsley on top. Season with salt and pepper. Serve the dressing separately in a small jug.

Serves 4
Preparation time: 20 minutes

Sweet Pepper Dressing

You could use peppers of any colour, but I prefer the vibrant tone that red peppers give.

2 red peppers
1 garlic clove, crushed
1 teaspoon paprika
½ teaspoon mustard powder
4 teaspoons red wine vinegar
125 ml/4 fl oz light olive oil
salt and pepper

1 Cook the peppers under a pre-heated hot grill for 15-20 minutes, turning occasionally, until the skin is blistered and blackened all over. Transfer to a bowl, cover with layers of kitchen paper and set aside.
2 When cool enough to handle, rub off and discard the charred skins. Cut each pepper in half and remove the seeds. Roughly chop the flesh.
3 Place the grilled pepper flesh in a liquidizer or food processor. Add the garlic, paprika, mustard and vinegar, with salt and pepper to taste. Process until fairly smooth.
4 With the motor running slowly, carefully pour in the oil until the dressing is smooth. Adjust the seasoning to taste.

Makes 300 ml/½ pint
Preparation time: 5 minutes
Cooking time: 15-20 minutes

Grated Carrots with Oranges and Walnut Dressing

375 g/12 oz large carrots
(peeled weight)
2 oranges
1 tablespoon walnut oil
about 6 tablespoons Walnut Dressing
(see page 42)
2 tablespoons chopped fresh herbs (e.g.
parsley, chervil, dill, chives)
salt and pepper

1 Cut the carrots into matchsticks and place in a large bowl. Grate the rind from 1 of the oranges and add to the bowl. Toss well.
2 Using a small sharp knife, cut away the rind and pith from both of the oranges, then cut the flesh into segments, leaving behind any skin or pith. This is best done over a bowl to catch the juice. Set aside.
3 Heat the oil in a large frying pan, add the carrots and cook, stirring, for 2 minutes; they should still be crisp. Transfer to a salad bowl and leave to cool.

4 To serve, add the orange segments, with their juice, to the salad bowl. Spoon over the dressing and season with salt and pepper. Toss lightly and sprinkle with the chopped herbs.

Serves 4
Preparation time: 10 minutes
Cooking time: 2 minutes

Roasted Parsnips Dressed with Lemon and Garlic

750 g/1½ lb parsnips
6 tablespoons extra-virgin olive oil
1 tablespoon roughly chopped fresh thyme
1 teaspoon finely grated lemon rind
2 tablespoons lemon juice
1 garlic clove, crushed
coarse sea salt and pepper
TO SERVE:
rocket or other salad leaves (optional)
50 g/2 oz Parmesan cheese (optional)

1 Cut the parsnips into 'batons' – lengths of about 5 cm x 1 cm (2 x ½ inch). Add to a pan of boiling water and parboil for 4 minutes. Drain well and leave to dry.

2 Transfer the parsnips to a roasting tin large enough to hold them in a single layer. Spoon the olive oil over the parsnips and then sprinkle with the thyme. Toss to coat. Place in a preheated oven, 200°C (400°F), Gas Mark 6, and roast for 45-60 minutes, stirring occasionally, until the parsnips are tender and lightly patched with brown. Transfer the cooked parsnips to a bowl and leave to cool slightly.

3 Add the lemon rind and juice and the garlic to the parsnips and season with coarse sea salt and pepper. Toss well and leave to cool.

4 Serve the dressed parsnips either as they are, or on a bed of rocket or other salad leaves. If liked, sprinkle wafer-thin shavings of Parmesan, pared with a potato peeler or a small sharp knife, over the parsnips.

Serves 4-6
Preparation time: 15 minutes
Cooking time: 45-60 minutes
Oven temperature: 200°C (400°F), Gas Mark 6

PASTA AND GRAINS

Fresh Apricot and Rice Salad with Grilled Goats' Cheese

Grilling goats' cheese brings out its flavour. Add a mixture of rice, apricots and almonds and you have a tasty and unusual first-course salad. For a lunch or supper dish serve the grilled cheese on a generous bed of salad leaves.

175 g/6 oz cooked white or brown rice
2 tablespoons finely chopped fresh parsley
1 tablespoon finely chopped fresh mint
1 quantity Classic French Dressing (see page 54)
6 large ripe apricots, halved and stoned
2 tablespoons chopped toasted almonds
4 thick slices of goats' cheese log, with rind
salt and pepper
sprigs of fresh herbs or salad leaves (e.g. sage, salad burnet), to garnish

1 Combine the rice and herbs in a bowl. Add 4 tablespoons of the dressing, with salt and pepper to taste. Mix well. Reserve the remaining dressing in a jug.
2 Fill the apricot cavities with the rice salad, piling it up in the centre. Arrange on individual serving plates. Scatter the toasted almonds over.
3 Place the goats' cheese slices on a baking sheet. Cook under a preheated hot grill for 3-4 minutes, until bubbling and patched with brown. Lift on to the serving plates and serve at once. Garnish with fresh herbs or salad leaves. Hand the remaining dressing around separately at the table.

Serves 4
Preparation time: 15 minutes
Cooking time: 3-4 minutes

Flageolet Bean and Roasted Vegetable Salad

1 aubergine, topped and tailed
1 red pepper, halved, cored and
  deseeded
1 yellow pepper, halved, cored and
  deseeded
1 courgette, topped and tailed
4 garlic cloves, peeled but left whole
4 tablespoons olive oil
1 teaspoon coarse sea salt
300 g/10 oz flageolet beans, cooked
  and drained
2 tablespoons chopped mixed herbs
  (parsley and oregano; or coriander
  and mint)
6 tablespoons Classic French Dressing
  (see page 54)
pepper

1 Cut all the vegetables into strips
and place in a roasting tin. Add the
garlic. Sprinkle over the oil, sea salt
and pepper. Place in a preheated
oven, 200°C (400°F), Gas Mark 6,
and roast for 40 minutes. Transfer to
a shallow bowl and leave to cool.
2 Add the beans and toss lightly. Stir
the herbs into the French dressing;
pour over the salad and serve.

Serves 4
Preparation time: 20 minutes
Cooking time: 40 minutes
Oven temperature: 200°C (400°F),
Gas Mark 6

Pasta with Roasted Tomatoes and Basil

Don't be alarmed by the amount of garlic used in this recipe. Slow-roasting tempers the flavour to a mild creaminess. Roasting the tomatoes, on the other hand, really concentrates their flavour.

20 cherry tomatoes
8 garlic cloves, peeled but left whole
2 teaspoons coarse sea salt
1 tablespoon chopped fresh thyme
375 g/12 oz dried tagliatelle or pasta bows (farfalle)
1 tablespoon olive oil
about 16 black olives
handful of shredded basil leaves
1 quantity Classic French Dressing (see page 54)
pepper

1 Halve the tomatoes. Arrange, cut side up, on a baking sheet. Tuck the garlic cloves among them and sprinkle over the salt, pepper and thyme. Roast in a preheated oven, 190°C (375°F), Gas Mark 5, for 45 minutes, until the tomatoes are soft, wrinkled and have lost much of their moisture. Leave to cool. Remove the garlic and set aside in a small bowl; mash lightly.
2 Bring a large saucepan of water to the boil, add the pasta and cook until just tender, 10-12 minutes. Drain in a colander and rinse under cold running water. Drain thoroughly and place in a large salad bowl. Add the olive oil and toss well.
3 Add the cooled roasted tomatoes to the pasta with the olives and basil. Stir the dressing into the mashed garlic, mix well and pour over the salad. Toss lightly.

Serves 4
Preparation time: 25 minutes
Cooking time: about 45 minutes
Oven temperature: 190°C (375°F), Gas Mark 5

Chinese Noodle and Prawn Salad

Chinese noodles are quick and easy to prepare, and make a very good basis for this pretty salad.

175 g/6 oz Chinese egg noodles
6 spring onions
1 small bunch of radishes, trimmed
175 g/6 oz sugar snap peas, topped and tailed

175 g/6 oz cooked peeled prawns
1 quantity Ginger and Lime Dressing (see page 90) or Sweet and Sour Dressing (see right)
salt and pepper

1 Bring a saucepan of water to the boil, add the noodles, cover the pan and remove from the heat. Leave to stand for 5 minutes, or until the noodles are just tender. Drain in a colander and cool under cold running water. Drain well and transfer to a salad bowl.
2 Meanwhile, cut the spring onions into short lengths and shred finely. Leave the radishes whole or cut them into slices, as preferred. Add both the spring onions and the radishes to the noodles.
3 Bring a saucepan of water to the boil, add the sugar snap peas and blanch for 1 minute. Drain in a colander, refresh under cold running water, then drain thoroughly. Add to the salad with the prawns. Season with salt and pepper to taste.
4 Just before serving add the chosen dressing to the salad and toss lightly.

Serves 4-6
Preparation time: 15 minutes
Cooking time: about 6 minutes

Sweet and Sour Dressing

Plums give this dressing a fresh, tangy flavour. Try it with a ham salad or a simple salad of mixed leaves tossed with hot grilled bacon.

1 spring onion
2 fresh ripe plums, stoned and finely diced
5 tablespoons olive or groundnut oil
2 tablespoons sherry vinegar
2 teaspoons soy sauce
2 teaspoons tomato purée
½ clove garlic, crushed
¼ teaspoon soft light brown sugar
salt and pepper

1 Cut the spring onion into fine shreds about 2.5 cm (1 inch) long. Place in a small bowl or screw-top jar. Add the diced plums.
2 Add the remaining ingredients to the bowl or jar and either whisk together with a fork or shake in the closed jar until combined. Use the dressing as required.

Makes about 250 ml/8 fl oz
Preparation time: 10 minutes

Fragrant Moulded Rice Salad

4 teaspoons groundnut or sunflower oil,
   plus extra for oiling tin
250 g/8 oz Thai fragrant rice
450 ml/¾ pint water
8-12 large spinach leaves
1 large carrot
1 large courgette
2 spring onions
2 tablespoons chopped fresh coriander
1 quantity Sweet Pepper Dressing (see
   page 103)
salt and pepper
nasturtium leaves, to garnish (optional)

1 Prepare a 500 g/1 lb loaf tin by brushing it with oil. Combine the rice and measured water in a small saucepan. Bring to the boil, then lower the heat and stir once. Cover the pan and simmer gently for 10 minutes, until the rice is tender and all the water has been absorbed. Remove the pan from the heat, allow to stand for 5 minutes, then fork through and allow to cool.
2 Meanwhile, half fill a large frying pan with water and bring to the boil. Add the spinach leaves and blanch briefly, until wilted. Drain, then spread the spinach leaves out on a clean tea towel to dry.
3 Using a potato peeler, pare the carrot and courgette into ribbons. Shred the spring onions into similar lengths. Heat the oil in a frying pan and sauté the vegetables over a

moderate heat for 3-4 minutes, stirring until tender. Remove the pan from the heat and season the vegetables with salt and pepper.
4 Line the prepared loaf tin with the wilted spinach leaves, overlapping them slightly and allowing them to hang over the top of the tin. Reserve any remaining leaves.
5 Add the coriander to the rice, with salt and pepper to taste. Mix well. Spoon half the rice mixture into the lined loaf tin, pressing down lightly. Arrange the vegetables in a layer on top. Spoon the remaining rice over the vegetables and press down lightly. Cover with the overlapping

spinach and any remaining spinach leaves to enclose completely.
6 Cover the rice mould with grease-proof paper or clingfilm and top with a weight. Chill the moulded salad for at least 30 minutes before turning out on a board or platter.
7 Cut the rice mould into 6 thick slices. Arrange on individual plates and serve with the sweet pepper dressing. Garnish with nasturtium leaves, if liked.

Serves 6
Preparation time: 30 minutes, plus chilling time
Cooking time: about 15 minutes

Green Lentils with Pancetta and Plum Tomatoes

If you cannot get pancetta for this salad a mixture of smoked streaky bacon and Italian salami can be used instead, with delicious results.

175 g/6 oz green (continental) lentils
175 g/6 oz pancetta, sliced
3 tablespoons extra-virgin olive oil
375 g/12 oz plum tomatoes, sliced
½ red onion, chopped
2 tablespoons chopped fresh parsley
salt and pepper
DRESSING:
4 tablespoons extra-virgin olive oil
2 tablespoons red wine vinegar
pinch of sugar
1 garlic clove, crushed

1 Put the lentils in a sieve and rinse under cold running water. Tip into a saucepan, cover with fresh water and bring to the boil. Boil rapidly for 10 minutes, then skim off any foam. Lower the heat, cover and simmer for 15-20 minutes, or until the lentils are just tender. Drain, rinse under cold running water, then drain again thoroughly. Transfer to a shallow serving bowl.
2 Cut the pancetta into short thin strips. Heat the oil in a large frying pan, add the pancetta and cook over a moderately high heat until it is beginning to crisp. Remove the pan from the heat.
3 Add the sliced tomatoes and chopped red onion to the lentils with the pancetta and parsley. Season with salt and pepper.
4 Just before serving place all the dressing ingredients in a small bowl and whisk until blended. Alternatively mix in a screw-top jar, close the lid tightly and shake until combined. Pour the dressing over the salad and toss to mix.

Serves 4
Preparation time: 20 minutes
Cooking time: 25-30 minutes

Long Fusilli with Asparagus, Peas and Lemon

Long fusilli – twisted lengths of pasta – are attractively shaped but you could use other pasta shapes such as penne or farfalle.

250 g/8 oz dried long fusilli
375 g/12 oz asparagus spears, trimmed and cut into 5 cm/2 inch lengths
125 g/4 oz frozen peas, thawed
2 large tomatoes, skinned, deseeded and chopped

small handful of basil leaves, torn
small handful of parsley leaves, torn
1 small lemon
1 quantity Classic French Dressing (see page 54)
salt and pepper

1 Bring a large saucepan of water to the boil, add the pasta and cook until just tender, about 10-12 minutes. Drain in a colander and rinse under cold running water. Drain thoroughly and transfer to a serving bowl.

2 Cook the asparagus in a shallow saucepan of boiling water for 4-5 minutes, until almost tender. Drain in a colander, cool under cold running water, then drain thoroughly. Add to the pasta.

3 Add the peas, tomatoes, basil and parsley to the pasta. Use a zester, if possible, to remove the outer rind from the lemon in thin narrow strips; add these to the salad. Season well with salt and pepper.

4 Just before serving squeeze the juice from the lemon and add to the salad with the dressing. Toss lightly.

Serves 4-6
Preparation time: 15 minutes
Cooking time: about 15 minutes

VARIATIONS

Long Fusilli with Leeks, Peas and Lemon

When asparagus is expensive or if it's not easy to buy, try using leeks as an alternative. Use 750 g/1½ lb leeks. Cut the leeks in half lengthways, then cut again lengthways into quarters to give long 'ribbons'. Cook these in boiling water as for the asparagus in step 2, but for about 2 minutes only, until just tender. Refresh under cold running water, drain thoroughly and add to the pasta as in the main recipe.

Long Fusilli with Asparagus, Lemon and Smoked Trout

Make the salad as for the main recipe, but add 250 g/8 oz smoked trout fillets. Flake the trout into the salad just before serving.

Pasta and Olive Salad with Quails' Eggs

Most of the olives in this salad are used to make a rich paste which coats the pasta to give a robust flavour.

250 g/8 oz dried pasta twists or quills (fusilli or penne rigate)
2 tablespoons olive oil
1 small onion or shallot, chopped
1 garlic clove, crushed
1 tablespoon chopped fresh oregano or parsley
175 g/6 oz pitted olives (preferably anchovy-stuffed)
1 tablespoon lemon juice
12 quails' eggs
6 tablespoons Mayonnaise (see page 15)
salt and pepper

1 Bring a large saucepan of water to the boil, add the pasta and cook until just tender. Drain in a colander and rinse under cold running water. Drain thoroughly and transfer to a large salad bowl.
2 Heat the oil in a small frying pan. Add the onion or shallot and cook for 3-4 minutes, until softened but not browned. Stir in the garlic and cook for 1 minute more. Stir in the oregano or parsley. Transfer the contents of the pan to a liquidizer or food processor.

3 Reserve 6-8 olives. Add the rest to the liquidizer or food processor with the lemon juice. Process for a few seconds, until the mixture forms a coarse paste.
4 Scrape the olive paste into the bowl with the pasta. Roughly chop the reserved olives and add to the bowl. Toss well. Season with pepper; the olives will be salty, so take care when seasoning.
5 Bring a small saucepan of water to the boil, add the quails' eggs and

cook for 3 minutes. Drain, refresh under cold running water and drain again. Remove the shells and halve the eggs. Arrange on the salad or on the side if serving individual portions.
6 Thin the mayonnaise to a pouring consistency with a little cold water. Add salt and pepper to taste, drizzle over the salad and serve.

Serves 4-6
Preparation time: 15 minutes
Cooking time: 18-20 minutes

Pepper and Rice Salad with Omelette Ribbons

2 red peppers, halved and deseeded
1 yellow pepper, halved and deseeded
1 onion
250 g/8 oz cooked rice (white or brown or a mixture)
salt and pepper
fresh herbs, to garnish
OMELETTE:
3 eggs
2 tablespoons chopped fresh herbs (e.g. parsley, dill, chives, chervil)
1 tablespoon light oil
DRESSING:
4 tablespoons crème fraîche or fromage frais
2 tablespoons olive oil
1 tablespoon white wine vinegar

1 Place the peppers skin side up on a grill rack. Cut the onion into quarters, leaving the root ends intact so that the layers do not separate. Add to the grill rack. Cook under a preheated hot grill for 10-15 minutes, until the peppers are blistered and blackened all over. Turn the onion wedges occasionally if necessary, but let them char a little. Remove the onions from the grill and leave to cool on a plate. Transfer the peppers to a bowl, cover with several layers of kitchen paper and set aside.
2 When cool enough to handle, rub off and discard the charred skin from the peppers; cut the flesh into thin strips. Roughly chop the onion. Combine the pepper and onion in a bowl. Add the cooked rice, with salt and pepper to taste. Toss lightly.
3 Make the omelette. Lightly beat the eggs in a bowl with the herbs and a little salt and pepper. Heat the oil in a large frying pan and pour in the egg mixture. Cook over moderate heat. While the surface is still slightly creamy, slide the omelette on to a board and roll it up like a Swiss roll. Leave to cool.

4 Make the dressing by stirring all the ingredients together in a small bowl. Pile the rice mixture on to individual serving plates. Slice the omelette roll and arrange the ribbons on top of the salad. Drizzle the dressing over and garnish with a sprinkling of fresh herbs.

Serves 4
Preparation time: 25 minutes
Cooking time: about 20 minutes

Wild Rice, Orange and Walnut Salad

Wild rice is not a rice at all, but the seeds of a grass that grows wild in North America and parts of China. It has a marvellous nutty flavour.

250 g/8 oz wild rice
2 small oranges
1 small fennel bulb, trimmed and thinly
   sliced
3 spring onions, finely chopped

50 g/2 oz walnut pieces
1 quantity Walnut Dressing (see
   page 42)
salt and pepper
chopped fennel tops, to garnish

1 Bring a large saucepan of water to the boil. Add the rice, lower the heat and simmer for about 30 minutes, or until tender. Drain the rice in a colander, refresh under cold running water, then drain thoroughly. Transfer the rice to a large salad bowl.
2 Using a small sharp knife, peel away the skin and all the pith from the oranges. Slice them as thinly as possible and add to the rice with the sliced fennel and spring onions.
3 Spread the walnuts on a baking sheet and toast under a preheated hot grill for 1-2 minutes, until they are lightly browned. Add to the salad, with salt and pepper to taste.
4 Pour the dressing over the salad and toss lightly. Sprinkle with chopped fennel tops to garnish.

Serves 4
Preparation time: 25 minutes
Cooking time: about 30 minutes

Pasta Primavera Salad

Fresh young spring vegetables are used in this pasta salad. Mangetout, French beans, courgettes or baby fennel give equally good results.

375 g/12 oz dried wide ribbon pasta
   (tagliatelle or pappardelle)
2 tablespoons light olive oil
175 g/6 oz tiny baby carrots
175 g/6 oz thin asparagus spears
175 g/6 oz sugar snap peas
175 g/6 oz cauliflower or broccoli
   florets
125 g/4 oz baby broad beans
handful of fresh herbs (e.g. chives, dill,
   fennel, parsley, tarragon),
   roughly chopped
1 quantity Garlic and Herb Mayonnaise
   (see page 95)
salt and pepper

1 Bring a large saucepan of water to the boil, add the pasta and cook for 10-12 minutes, until just tender. Drain in a colander and rinse under cold running water. Drain thoroughly and transfer to a large salad bowl. Add the olive oil and toss well.
2 Prepare all the spring vegetables, trimming away as little as possible. Cook briefly in a saucepan of boiling water, until the vegetables are just tender, but retain their crispness. Drain, refresh under cold running water, then drain again. Pat the vegetables dry on kitchen paper to blot off excess moisture, but do not leave the vegetables on the kitchen paper for any length of time because it will soak up all the natural juices. Add the cooked spring vegetables to the pasta with the herbs and salt and pepper to taste.
3 Stir a little cold water into the mayonnaise to thin it to a thick pouring consistency. Pour the mayonnaise over the salad, toss lightly and serve.

Serves 4-6
Preparation time: 20-25 minutes
Cooking time: about 5 minutes

Spiced Dhal Salad with Yogurt Dressing

Red lentils combined with cumin, coriander and cayenne make a spicy salad served with a yogurt cooler.

375 g/12 oz red lentils
1 bay leaf
2 teaspoons cumin seeds, finely crushed
2 teaspoons coriander seeds, finely crushed
pinch of cayenne pepper
600 ml/1 pint water
6 tablespoons olive oil
2 onions, finely sliced
2 garlic cloves, chopped
1 tablespoon lemon juice
1 quantity Yogurt Dressing (see page 38)
salt and pepper
chopped fresh coriander, to garnish

1 Combine the red lentils, bay leaf, spices and measured water in a saucepan. Add salt and pepper to taste. Bring to the boil, then lower the heat, cover and simmer for about 15 minutes, or until the lentils are just tender and most of the water has been absorbed. Drain the lentil mixture, discarding the bay leaf, and transfer to a shallow serving bowl. Leave to cool.

2 Heat the oil in a large frying pan. Add the onions and cook, stirring occasionally, over a moderately high heat for 5 minutes. Stir in the garlic and continue to cook until the onions start to brown and caramelize.

3 Drizzle the oil from the frying pan over the lentils. Add the lemon juice and toss lightly. Spoon a little of the yogurt dressing on to the salad and pile the onions on top. Garnish with a sprinkling of fresh coriander. Serve the remaining dressing separately at the table.

Serves 4-6
Preparation time: 10 minutes
Cooking time: 20-25 minutes

Pasta and Avocado Salad with Tomato Dressing

The salsa-like dressing is the perfect foil for pasta and avocados in this summery salad. The salad is simplicity itself and can be prepared at a moment's notice, particularly easy since most of the ingredients (there aren't many anyway) are staple store cupboard items. Although pasta shells look very attractive any shape of pasta can be used as an alternative.

175 g/6 oz small pasta shells
1 quantity Tomato, Garlic and Summer
  Herb Dressing (see right)

2 ripe avocados
salt and pepper

1 Bring a large saucepan of water to the boil, add the pasta and cook until just tender to the bite. Drain in a colander and rinse under cold running water. Drain thoroughly and transfer to a bowl.
2 Add the dressing to the pasta and toss well, to coat the pasta completely. Season with salt and pepper.
3 Just before serving, halve and stone the avocados. Peel and slice them, then arrange on individual serving plates. Divide the dressed pasta salad between the plates.

Serves 4
Preparation time: 10 minutes
Cooking time: 10-12 minutes

Tomato, Garlic and Summer Herb Dressing

Try this dressing with pasta, rice and grain salads, with cheeses or grilled lamb, chicken or fish. It also makes a good dressing for summer vegetable salads based on avocado, asparagus or beans.

500 g/1 lb ripe tomatoes, skinned, deseeded and finely diced
2 garlic cloves, finely chopped
2 tablespoons balsamic vinegar
4 tablespoons extra-virgin olive oil
6 large basil leaves, finely shredded
3 tablespoons chopped mixed fresh herbs (e.g. oregano, dill, chervil, chives, parsley, mint)
salt and pepper

1 Place the tomatoes in a bowl with the garlic, balsamic vinegar and olive oil. Stir well.
2 Add the shredded basil to the tomato mixture with the mixed herbs. Stir in salt and pepper to taste. Mix thoroughly. Leave to stand for at least 30 minutes before using, to allow the flavours to develop and mingle.

Makes 350 ml/12 fl oz
Preparation time: 15 minutes

Wholewheat Salad with Orange and Date

The combination of grain, celery, oranges and dates proves highly successful. Try to find very fresh crisp celery and soft, succulent dates for a good contrast of textures.

175 g/6 oz dried wholewheat, soaked overnight
4 celery sticks, very thinly sliced
1 tablespoon chopped fresh sage or tarragon
2 oranges
175 g/6 oz fresh dates, pitted and chopped
salt and pepper
1 quantity Walnut Dressing (see page 42) or Tarragon and Orange Dressing (see page18)

1 Drain the wholewheat in a very fine sieve, tip it into a saucepan and cover completely with plenty of fresh cold water. Bring to the boil, then lower the heat and simmer for about 20-25 minutes, or until just tender. Drain in a colander, rinse under cold running water, then drain thoroughly. Transfer the drained wholewheat to a large salad bowl and then leave to cool completely.
2 Add the celery to the wholewheat in the bowl, together with the chopped fresh sage or tarragon.

3 Using a small sharp knife, carefully cut away the skin and all the pith from the oranges. Cut the flesh into segments and add to the salad, together with the chopped fresh dates. Toss lightly to combine the ingredients evenly, then season with salt and pepper to taste.

4 Pour the chosen dressing over the salad and toss to mix.

Serves 4-6
Preparation time: 25 minutes
Cooking time: 20-25 minutes

Bean Salad with Grilled Onion

Char-grilled onions add flavour to this substantial salad.

250 g/8 oz dried cannellini beans, soaked overnight
2 large or 3 smaller red or mild white onions
DRESSING:
150 ml/¼ pint light olive oil
5 tablespoons lemon juice
2 garlic cloves, crushed
2 tablespoons finely chopped fresh parsley
pinch of mustard powder
pinch of sugar
salt and pepper

1 Drain the beans, then tip them into a saucepan. Cover with plenty of fresh water and bring to the boil. Boil rapidly for 10 minutes, then lower the heat, cover and simmer for 40-50 minutes, or until tender. Drain in a colander, rinse under cold running water, then drain thoroughly again. Transfer to a serving bowl and set aside until cold.
2 Meanwhile, prepare the dressing by whisking all the ingredients together in a small bowl. Alternatively place them in a screw-top jar, close the lid tightly and shake until combined.
3 Cut the onions into wedges, keeping the root ends intact so that the layers do not separate. Place on a grill rack and brush each wedge with a little of the dressing. Cook under a preheated moderately hot grill for about 8 minutes, until the onions are tender and beginning to char. Leave to cool.
4 Pile the onion wedges on top of the cold beans. Pour the remaining dressing over the salad and serve.

Serves 4
Preparation time: 20 minutes, plus overnight soaking
Cooking time: about 1 hour

Saffron Barley with Sun-dried Tomatoes and Oyster Mushrooms

Sun-dried tomatoes are a real gift for the salad maker. With their concentrated flavour they make a very good addition to this barley and mushroom mixture.

250 g/8 oz pearl barley
750 ml/1¼ pints chicken or vegetable stock
¼ teaspoon saffron threads
6 tablespoons olive oil
1 shallot, finely chopped
1 garlic clove, crushed

375 g/12 oz oyster mushrooms, trimmed, halved if large
8-12 sun-dried tomatoes preserved in oil, drained and chopped
handful of basil leaves, shredded
2 tablespoons white wine vinegar
salt and pepper

1 Put the pearl barley in a large saucepan with the stock. Crumble in the saffron. Bring to the boil, then lower the heat, cover the pan and simmer for 20-25 minutes, until all the liquid is absorbed. Transfer the pearl barley to a shallow serving bowl and leave to cool.

2 Meanwhile, heat 3 tablespoons of the olive oil in a large frying pan. Add the shallot and cook over a moderate heat for about 3 minutes, until softened. Stir in the garlic and mushrooms and cook for a further 3 minutes, until tender. Remove from the heat and stir in the sun-dried tomatoes and basil. Use a slotted spoon to remove the mushroom mixture from the pan and pile it on top of the barley. Leave to cool.

3 Add the remaining olive oil to the frying pan but do not heat. Stir in the white wine vinegar, with salt and pepper to taste. Spoon the dressing over the salad to serve.

Serves 4
Preparation time: 15-20 minutes, plus standing time
Cooking time: about 30 minutes

VARIATIONS

Saffron Barley, Seafood and Herb Salad

For a delicious seafood salad replace the sun-dried tomatoes and oyster mushrooms with 500 g/1 lb frozen seafood salad, thawed, and 3 tablespoons fresh chopped mixed herbs such as dill, chives and parsley. Add the pared rind of 1 small lemon to the salad and use the rest of the lemon, cut into wedges, as a garnish.

Barley Pearls with Mangetout and Oyster Mushrooms

Omit the saffron and the sun-dried tomatoes. Increase the garlic to 2 cloves. When cooking the mushrooms, add 175 g/6 oz trimmed mangetout to the pan. Continue as for the main recipe.